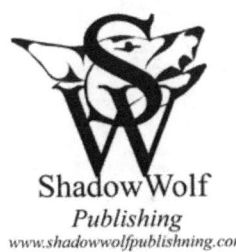

Shadow Wolf
Publishing
www.shadowwolfpublishning.com

The $even $teps to $elling Your Artwork

By Jane Croy

Notice

The information in this book has been carefully researched, and all efforts have been made to ensure accuracy. Shadow Wolf Publishing assumes no responsibility for any injuries suffered or damages or losses incurred during or as a result of following this information. All information should be carefully studied and clearly understood before taking any action based on the information or advice in this book.

   Mention of specific companies, organizations or authorities in this book does not imply endorsement by the publisher, nor does mention of specific companies, organizations, or authorities imply that they endorse the book.

   Internet addresses, addresses, and contact information given in this book were accurate at the time it went to press.

ISBN 978-1460911488

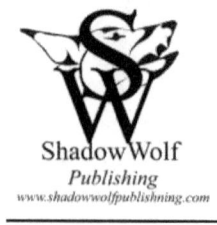

Shadow Wolf
Publishing
www.shadowwolfpublishning.com

Dedicated to all aspiring artists on their way to renown

Table of Contents

Introduction/A Four Letter Word

About four years ago, I went to New York for the first time, traveling with a group of students from the local art college. To fill up spaces on the trip, adult artists were given an opportunity to join the students as they saw what the "Big Apple" had to offer in the way of past art, current art and the cutting edge of future art. All total, there were about 42 young (late teens and early 20's) students and about 8-10 adults, counting one adult student and adult teacher/sponsors.

The trip was wonderful! Great weather and comfortable shoes allowed me to see art, art, and more art. I visited every major art gallery, many minor art galleries (which seemed to be everywhere), art schools, and I even got the opportunity to "visit" art galleries from around the world. You see, it just so happened that The Armory Show was scheduled while I was there. This show filled two piers on the west side of New York which were set up for displays of artwork from galleries around the world.

One year prior to this trip, I had opened an art gallery myself. The main purpose of this trip was to see how the art in my gallery compared to the art in New York. What I found pleasantly surprised me! With the exception of conceptual pieces (like six inner tubes painted gold and set up in the middle of the floor), I found that the artwork in my gallery was as good as almost any of the current showings in any gallery in the world. The only difference was price. The prices on the artwork in my gallery were much lower compared to the prices in New York and around the world.

That was one thing I learned from my trip. The second thing I learned had to do with marketing your art and the purpose of this book.

Before the trip began, with permission of the trip's sponsors, I met with all of the students that were going on the trip and offered each student a chance to recoup some of the trip's expense by having a group show in my gallery. Following the trip, each student would be allowed to not only show but to sell some of their artwork. As a college assignment, each student was required to keep a sketchbook of the trip from which they were to create at least one completed work of art. These pieces were to be shown at the college about one month after the trip and were created as a grade for one of their classes. My offer was to allow them, during the month following the school show, to bring those pieces and any other pieces inspired by the trip to the gallery for a chance to sell some of their work. I even encouraged them to bring their sketchbooks for display so that the gallery guests could see where a painting or work of art often starts and to get an idea of how it proceeds to its final showing.

This was a wonderful show idea for my gallery. I even offered the same opportunity to the adult artists who were tagging along on this trip.

Assuming that the students would be excited about the chance to actually reach the public with their artwork . . . much less, having a chance to sell a few pieces for perhaps the

2

first time in their life. . . I set about to publicize the show. As time grew closer for delivery of the pieces, I began to get more and more phone calls expressing excitement from the adult artists. Some even brought pieces by to show me how far along their ideas were coming. These artists had worked with a gallery before. They knew the importance of the knowledge of a gallery representative and were attempting to fine tune their pieces for some serious sales.

Of the eight adult artists who went on the trip, all eight submitted one or more pieces for the show. Of the 42 students, only one submitted work for the show! One day after the date for submissions I called the teacher who had allowed me to present this opportunity to the students. His only response to me was "I'm sorry". He went on to explain that the students had done their assignments and that he had reminded them of the opportunity to show at the gallery but once the class assignment was over, the students had made a mad dash for summer break, leaving their artwork hanging on walls or stored in studios.

My gallery consisted of more than 750 linear feet of showroom space and with so few New York inspired pieces to show I was forced to fill the rest of the showroom with old pieces from my represented artists. I still featured our "New York, New York" show but in a smaller corner of the gallery. And, by the way, we sold about a third of the New York themed pieces.

Upon further reflection as to how these students could turn down a "gift horse" (the opportunity to show their work in a "real" gallery) I thought back to my college days. Majoring in art and art education, I can remember that in the 70's we were still young "hippies" bucking the establishment. Art students fought hard against the norm. We fought against working for the "man" and were taught to create art for art's sake – not for the specific purpose of sales. I can't remember a time that marketing or selling one's artwork ever came up in the classroom. Since my degree was to be in art education, I had grandiose ideas of inspiring every young artist who came my way and even   I hadn't thought much of art marketing either. I wasn't planning on selling my art, just creating art so that I could instruct others to create art. I guess I just thought that sales came naturally,   sort of an "if you paint it, they will come" attitude.   I can remember the fine art majors exemplifying the look of the "starving artist".   I studied the lives of artists who lived and died creating art that would later sell for hundreds of thousands of dollars but during their lifetimes was traded for a meager meal or a roof over their heads; artists who shunned the world of status quo for a deserted desert isle.

No one anywhere had even mentioned that horrible four letter word, "S-E-L-L". We didn't talk about it, we didn't think about it, and heavens no, we didn't have a class to teach us anything about it.

What a rude awakening for the artists without the teaching job or any kind of day job to back them up! They created their artwork only to see it accumulate in their run down studio apartments after graduation.   They knew everything about

4

creating the artwork but nothing about how to sell or market that same artwork.

With my teaching degree in hand, I began to teach art to junior high students. I quickly realized that this was not where I wanted to be but having no back-up plan, I struggled through thirteen years of "don't sling the paint", "do not make tattoos with the India Ink", "no, you may not go to the restroom again", and many other comments that had nothing to do with creating art. Crowded classrooms and stubborn beaurocratic principals sent me job searching every summer. I spent time doing anything and everything I could do in art that might equal or come close to my teacher's salary. I painted signs, did murals, faux finished furniture and walls, worked with interior designers and even tried (horrors) to "sell" by own artwork. What I finally realized was that after "fighting" my art students all school year it was taking two months of my summer vacation to get my creative juices flowing again and then I had less than one month before school began again. My art work was haphazard and poorly presented and I knew it but I didn't have the motivation, time, knowledge, or inclination to make it better.

I had fallen into the paycheck "trap" and went back each of the thirteen years that I taught in the public school system with the idea that this year I would inspire, this year I would overcome the lackluster desire of junior high students to create art, this year I would be a shining beacon. And every summer I went looking for another art job. By the end of the third or fourth year, I began looking for another "any kind" of job only to find that an art education degree and a dollar wouldn't even get you a cup of coffee.

Disillusioned with teaching art, I also became disillusioned with even creating art. I left the art world for the glamorous life of the casinos (working in, not gambling at). The pay was comparable and it took relatively little "re-training" for someone with a master's degree to slap out cards on a Black Jack table.

Now, I'm a firm believer that everything you do in life, everywhere you go, if evaluated and used, teaches you something to become more successful in the next stages of your life. During the first five years that I spent in the casinos, I didn't pick up a brush or even a pencil to create art. In wondering if those years were wasted or if they were a necessary evil to learn something for the next stage of my life, I firmly believe that yes, they were learning years. Though I never picked up a brush, I "picked up" the knowledge of public relations and customer service which would prove invaluable in the art marketing world.

During the last two years of being in the casino business, I began doing sketches again and some of my co-workers saw them, exclaiming "man, if I could draw like that I sure wouldn't be in this business. I'd be an artist" and "man, you're good, you could sell your artwork" like as if I never thought of wanting to do that before. So the more I painted and drew, the more I began to agree that life in the casino business was going to be a dead end for me if I didn't do what my passion was calling me to do – to create art. And maybe, just maybe, I

6

could learn to sell a few pieces.

Testing the waters I began to spend my off days and early mornings before work creating new paintings. As time progressed I started working in faux finishes for an interior decoration firm. Along with the faux finishes came an opportunity to paint scenes on furniture and murals on walls. Along with murals and scenes came an order for a painting or two. Along with an order for a painting or two came a lady who owned a home and a vacation home both located in two active artistic communities. She began buying anything and everything that I could paint and reselling the pieces for a profit. After two years of this, painting and selling a minimum of one medium to large size painting a week, I began to gain both the skills and confidence to break out on my own.

Thus began the trial and error of marketing my own art and eventually the work of other artists, which I wish to share with you. My sincere desire is that you are able to find ease and comfort in the selling of your own art. I'm hoping the word "sell" doesn't become a dreaded four letter word but an accent to your creative process. My greatest desire is that selling will become a natural and comfortable progression to your art career. It's a left brained activity for an artistic right brained person so it's going to contradict almost everything your creative process tells you to do. But I have tried, in these pages, to show you a way to make it less painful and actually a little fun. I'm definitely going to make it easier for you. With this book you'll be getting a "jump start" not only from the knowledge gained from my own personal experiences but also from the knowledge of the experiences, both good and bad, of hundreds of fellow artists.   I've also taken this knowledge and divided it into seven actions or, if you will, seven steps to follow to become as successful as you can be in the marketing of your art.   I wish you the best of luck in your art career as you work toward becoming a professional "selling" artist.

Chapter 1/Step 1:Declare "I am an Artist!"

When I teach my art marketing classes, the first thing I do is to have everyone introduce themselves. It's a common activity in classes or seminars so no one is usually the wiser to know that I am listening for something specific from the students. I ask each of them to tell us their name and a little about themselves. As the name and information is given, I make note of one thing in particular . . . how many of the students actually call themselves an artist?

My marketing classes or seminars are always advertised as a class to market your art, so you would assume that most of the students would be artists. Most often, however, no one actually says "My name is 'so and so' and I am an artist". Since the class is usually made up of people who may just be beginning their art career (irregardless of how many years they have been creating art) they usually will tell the class about how they just retired, or they are a doctor, or lawyer, or Indian chief or whatever but seldom do they say that they are an "artist".

One of the main reasons for this is the false impression of the title, "artist". Most people feel that declaring oneself to be an artist is tantamount with declaring oneself to be a "movie star" or some other known celebrity. I even found it a little awkward myself when I first began calling myself an artist. There's something that sounds like bragging to call oneself an artist. When does one feel that he deserves the title of "artist"?

My answer is that if you create art, then you are an artist. There is no degree you must have or accomplishment that you must achieve in order to call yourself an artist. Granted even though you may call yourself an artist, you may be a "bad" artist just as an actor may be a "bad" actor but that doesn't make them any less an actor or you, any less an artist.

So, your first step to selling your art is a lesson in being able to say the words "I am an artist". At first it may sound silly to try to say these words but practice a little and it will begin to become more natural. To make it easier try saying "I am an artist working as a _____" (fill in the blank with your current career or the role you play in life like mother, or retiree, etc)". Whatever you do, though, make sure to say "I am an artist" first. For example don't say "I am a housewife but I'm trying to be an artist" or "I'm retired but I'm dabbling in art" or "I'm a doctor but I love to sculpt". If you are making an attempt at being a "real" artist, then you have to "talk the talk" in addition to "walking the walk". Remember, to sell art, you must first BE an artist.

Once you have the confidence to introduce yourself to others as an artist you will find some interesting things will begin to happen in your art career. First of all, if you have said something like, "I am an artist working as a waiter (or

10

whatever)" no one is really going to hear the second part of that statement. The vision that most people have when they think about the "artist" is that glamorous vision of the successful artist depicted in movies and books. You know the one. The artist in the fancy loft apartment, canvas draped over their easel, wining and dining on their latest commission or hob knobbing with everyone in high society, taking regular trips to Europe and loaded with paying commissions from collectors around the world. Thinking that your world is that glamorous, nine times out of ten the next question out of their mouths will be something like, "An artist? How fascinating! What kind of art do you do?"

The answer to this question should be relatively easy. If it's not, make it easy by answering rather broadly. Just say "I do paintings" whether you do watercolors, or oil paintings or mixed media or whatever. Just say "I do sculpture" whether it's ceramic or bronze or stone. Just say, "I'm a photographer." Part of answering briefly is to gauge your questioner as to whether they are really interested in what you do or if they are just making small talk. Don't get too detailed until the next question pops up which will usually go something like "Hmmmm, paintings. . .what kind of paintings?" and this is where you can make or break your artistic reputation.

Let's say you answer this last question with something like "Oh, I do watercolors but I've been working with acrylics since last Christmas when I got a set on sale" or "I mostly paint landscapes but I did a portrait of my nieces for my brother's birthday and I've been dying to try my hand at oil painting" or something just as long and drawn out. I can just about guarantee that you'll see the questioner's eyes glaze over as the mystique of your artistic profession turns into their vision of a dabbler in art who has no idea what they are doing.

To answer the question properly you need to be able to answer with "style". By this I don't mean a swish of your hand and an artistic gesture but an answer with a concrete, certifiable, genuine artistic style for your artwork. Here, then is where we begin our journey to becoming a successful "selling" artist.

Chapter 2/Step 2 – Practice R.A.D.

After close to three hours of writing time (I was on a roll) and just about the time I started to rub the back of my neck from bending over a "hot" computer all day, I get a pop up message that says "Microsoft has detected a problem and needs to close. Would you like to send a message to Microsoft about the problem?" Well, no, I didn't care to send the message since my laptop wasn't on line at the time but I would like to click "cancel" and then save my work before Microsoft closed down. You can guess the rest of the story. Microsoft closed down all right, but with not one nanosecond of time for me to save my work. Thus I am back at the computer today rethinking, rewording and re-researching to re-do the two chapters that were lost.

I share this with you for several reasons. First of all, the two chapters that I lost were so important to me that, even before editing, I had already begun to realize that I was talking way too much trying to emphasize my points. Therefore in getting it all out of my system the first time, I was able to make the next two chapters a little more exact and to the point just as you'll need to READ carefully to pin point the exact information from this book that is going to work for you in selling your artwork.

Secondly, I learned to have much more patience with my book just as you need to have patience to ASSIMILATE all the information that I'll be giving you even if some of it sounds more like common sense than anything revolutionary or new.

Third, as has been said in business seminars, "You may have heard all this before but the number one problem is that you aren't doing any of this at all". So I encourage moments to stop and DO in addition to reading and assimilating all this information.

Did you notice the capitalized words in the previous paragraphs? The initials to these words make up our next step in selling your artwork. READ, ASSIMILATE, and DO or as the abbreviation becomes - R.A.D.

RAD is so important. No matter what I try to teach you in these seven steps you will be productive only if you act on this learning. There have been a million times in my life I've heard information (from my parents to my college professors) and never acted, or worse yet, have gone contrary to that information. Disastrous or at least uncomfortable results often occurred.

How about you? How many "how to" books have you picked up, read, gathered knowledge and intended to use only to find that time slipped past without any action. You may have underlined, taken notes, filled out workbooks, but still to no benefit if no action was taken.

It's the same way in lectures and workshops. Tons of helpful information comes your way but if you don't understand, assimilate and then act on the information, all is in

14

vain.

That's why step 2, RAD (Reading, Assimilating, and Doing) is so important to the success of your art sales, art career and your art professionalism. If you just read, you'll get nowhere. If you understand what I have to say and remember it, you'll still get nowhere. It's a three part process for accomplishing something with the information that comes your way.

So just as I had to force myself to re-think and re-write the lost pages of my book, I encourage you to practice RAD throughout these pages. Read what I have to say, assimilate it by underlining, turning down pages, or making notes and then actually stop and do something. It can be as small as taking a good long look at your artwork or sorting out your colored pencils. It can be as important as setting down at the computer to write a resume or visiting your local art galleries. But whatever it is, as you study this and for that matter any other self-help book, apply RAD to your studies and you'll grow from your knowledge. Don't let the opportunities available to you slip by. Whether you use the knowledge from these seven steps or whether you are inspired to create your own plan from the assimilated ideas of several sources of information, the application of RAD is sure to help you succeed.

Throughout the pages of this book, you'll see the letters "RAD" just kind of stuck in here and there to remind you that this would be a good time to maybe stop and do something about what you just learned. Take advantage of the opportunity.   I'd love to see this book as dog eared and underlined and noted as you can make it as you read it, apply its steps to your artwork, and SELL THAT ART!

Chapter 3/Step 3 – Have Some Style

Why develop a style?

In my years as a gallery owner/curator, I have found that most of the beginning artists who bring work into my gallery bring a huge diversity of styles and/or subject matters and/or mediums into the gallery at one time.   I know what they are trying to do.   They are not sure what I am going to like or dislike and they bring everything but the kitchen sink in for me to see.   I have seen literally truck and trailer loads of paintings, sketchbooks, and sculptures at one time.

When asked why they've brought in so much artwork, most of the artists say that they bring all this work in so that I'll be able to see all of their talents and skills and the fact that   they can work in a variety of styles.   Has this been your philosophy?   Then it's time to make a change.

Let me pause here with a story that will hopefully emphasize my point better than almost anything else that I can say about the "why?" of style.

Let's say you want to buy a truck.   If you go to the local used car lot in the city you may find a truck or two to choose from but if you wanted a specific brand/size/style/color of truck at this location you might only have two to choose from. You could also go to a high end new car lot in the city and perhaps not see any trucks at all.   But let's say you drove out of town a little ways into the country. Undoubtedly here you would find a dealership with hundreds of new and used trucks from which to choose.   Now, you not only get to pick the brand, size, and model but there's a bunch of colors and different interiors and special features that you didn't even know you wanted until you saw them.

Or let's say you want to buy a really special bracelet for yourself or a friend . . . would you be more inclined to shop at a department store where you will pass clothes, furniture, appliances and makeup before you get to the jewelry counter or would you rather go straight to a jewelry store?   Probably the jewelry store because the selection will be better and possibly nicer and more unique.   Once at the jewelry store, will you stop to gaze longer at the case with necklaces, earrings, bracelets, and pendants all together or will you spend more time at the counter that is filled with nothing but bracelets?

So how does this relate to the style of your artwork? Picture this scenario – You are at a crafts show just browsing around.   How quickly do you walk past the booth filled with jewelry and handcrafted dolls and painted dishes and handmade brooms versus the booth with only handmade brooms (large and small, some with knotted wood handles and some with carved figurines on the handle), or the booth with only handcrafted dolls (large and small, some with elaborate outfits, some that look like babies and some in costumes of

18

other countries).

Are you getting the idea? If you show everything you are able to create, you are liable to lose people in the translation. They wanted a "bracelet" but you are showing them "necklaces" and "earrings" and "pendants" and oh, yes, by the way, you do have ONE bracelet that you can show them. If they didn't want any thing but the bracelet in the first place, then usually no amount of showing is going to convince them to change their mind. And with only one bracelet, it's going to be rare that it's just the right size, color and style they were looking for. Let's replace the word "bracelet" with the word "abstract painting" in the above example and fill in the assortment of items that you would show them like this – The prospective customer wants an abstract painting but you are showing them landscapes and portraits and oh, yes, by the way, you do have ONE abstract that you can show them. If they didn't want anything but the abstract in the first place, then usually no amount of showing is going to convince them to change their mind. And with only one abstract to show them, it's going to be rare that it's just the right size, color and style they were looking for. See what I mean?

Every beginning artist searches for what they like to paint or photograph or sculpt best. Every "BEGINNER" artist does this searching BUT customers and potential collectors seldom want the work of a "beginner" artist. And nothing says "beginner" more than someone obviously searching for their style, someone who seems to be a "jack of all trades but a master of none". In my experience as an artist and as a gallery owner I've found that most customers only need a little reinforcement that the work of art they are admiring is going to be a good purchase.   There's no way for them to tell if that decision is going to be a good one if you're a "beginner".

So even if YOU consider yourself a beginner, once you find your chosen style you'll easily cross the line into professionalism.   And a professional artist sells a lot more work than a beginner artist.

Now before we go on let me quell some arguments right here and now.   Sure you may know "so and so" who sells anything they can paint and they are just beginning and they'll swear they have no "style".   I've even met up with one or two of these "starving artist/beginner artists" myself, but I've met up with hundreds of artists so the odds are not in your favor to keep painting without a style.   And if you really look carefully at the work of those artists I bet you'll see a technique or medium or theme that is common to everything they do. That's a style whether they want to claim it or not.

Take a good look at your current inventory of artwork right now. (RAD) Do you see a style?   Or are you "all over the place" in subjects, themes, mediums and techniques?   Can you accurately answer this question yet?

"As an artist, what are you best known for?"

If you can't answer this question yet, maybe you just need to search a little more to find a style that's already there.

Where's your style?

Hopefully by now I have convinced you that painting everything in every way or photographing everything or sculpting everything in every medium is not the professional way to get your artwork sold. Right now you may be looking at your artwork and seeing a huge amount of diversity. Maybe you are trying to figure out what your style is exactly. Perhaps you are looking at your work and you actually think you see a glimmer of consistency among the themes or brushstrokes or colors.

Let's assume that you do see this glimmer of a style hiding in your creations already.   What is it?   How do you define it?

First of all, try grouping your artwork..   (RAD) Find enough space to spread it all out before you, picking out one piece at a time and categorizing it.   You may find it is similar in subject matter or color.   Perhaps it's similar in the use of texture or patterns.   Do you find that one group is larger than the others?   Do you favor one group over the others?   Keep these points in mind as you arrange and re-arrange.

Next you will try to match up your groups to a possible style. There are several ways to do this.

One way is to match your styles to the "masters" of the art world.   During some quiet time after your grouping, take out some of those old art history books you've got leftover from college. If you don't have any art history books you can check out some from your local library or purchase some from your local book store. Several good ones are suggested in the appendix of this book. Flip through the pages of one or two of these books to see if any of your groups match any particular time period of art.   See if your art tends to fit into a certain classification or style of art. As an added benefit, as you read these history books (RAD) you'll also pick up on words that will have greater meaning to you, your artwork and the art community with whom you are going to be involved.   Even if you don't know every name and date of every art period in the books, you'll begin to sound a lot more like you know what you're doing (sound more professional) when   given the opportunity to talk about your work just by doing a little light reading.

If you begin to   notice an art movement or time period or style that you feel resembles your artwork, take some time to read more about the artists themselves (RAD).   The biographies of artists can be very inspiring.   As you read, imagine which artists you would have felt most comfortable with.   Would you have enjoyed sitting around the table with Monet, Degas or Renoir or would you and Picasso have had a wonderful afternoon at the beach talking "shop"?

If you still can't figure out a style that "fits" your artwork consider the information I found in a recent local   art group's newsletter. The article took a fun look at some styles you might not have even heard of.   How about synchronism, orphism, rayonism, suprematism, vorticism or constructivism.   Yes, those are real styles.   Synchonism is a system in which meaning or significance does not rely on resemblance of the object. (Example: MacDonald-Wright, Morgan Russell) Orphism was a 1913 movement within cubism. Rayonism is a synthesis of cubism, futurism and orphism. The styles and their details can go on and on. Again, it's not important that you know each and every detail about every style but it's just fun to know that those styles are out there so if you are still searching enjoy the ride until you find out where your work "fits" in.

When you find a close "fit", enjoy the feeling of being a "part" of this style. Try out your declarative statement (RAD). Say something like, "I am an artist and I do paintings in the impressionistic style". Your style doesn't have to fit in perfectly and you may even be leaning a little toward your own uniqueness but there should be a basic style from which your style evolves.

Another way to find your style is to set up all your artwork and invite friends and neighbors over to see it (RAD) Invite the ones you really trust for their honest opinion. Ask them NOT to tell you how much they like your work but rather ask them this question:

What's my style?

Even if they don't know their art history lessons, they will probably come up with something. At first it may be rather generic like "Oh, you do abstracts" or "It's realism to me". You might even find that they will give you a whole new style category. That's how I found a style label for my artwork.

I already knew from my studies over the years and from

the work that I had been doing for so long that my style was impressionistic. Imagine my surprise when a fellow artist said, "Yes, they're impressionistic but sorta 'chunky impressionism'". Well, I thought about it and figured that she was on to something. Yes, I did impressionism but it wasn't the short small brush strokes of an old master. It was more like large bold strokes of color. I almost use my brush like a palette knife, applying multiple layers of color with little or no blending on the palette or the canvas. So, yes, "chunky impressionism" seemed to fit the bill and every time I say it to a potential customer they want to know more. Now, not only do I have my own style but because of its' uniqueness I am given even more opportunities to talk about my artwork.

Listen carefully and objectively to these friends and neighbors and then go back to the art history books to read up on the styles they may have suggested. (RAD)

Now, let's say that with books, friends, and family comments, and with all the studying that you can do, you still haven't come up with a definitive style. Perhaps you don't have one yet. So now, how do you get one?

How do I find a style?

The answer that I am going to tell you will be worth more than anything else that you may learn from reading this entire book. In other words, you are getting your money's worth right here when I tell you how to get your style. But it's

24

not gong to be the easy answer that you might be searching for. The answer to getting and knowing your style is to . . .

paint, paint, paint

sculpt, sculpt, sculpt

photograph, photograph, photograph

etc, etc, etc

Not exactly what you hoped for is it? But if you love what you do, then it's a "dirty job" but someone has to do it and you're going to love what it does for your artwork.

I speak from personal experience when I say that I was once that beginner artist who had work all over the place. I did watercolor landscapes, watercolor still lifes, acrylic murals, pencil sketches, pastel portraits, oil paintings, etc. I enjoyed doing so many things and for the sake of a hobby that was fine. But when I began to want to sell my work, no one knew who I was. No one knew my style including me.

Then one day, I was doing still another artistic endeavor as I worked on custom furniture for an interior decorator. One of the customers saw a small scene that I was painting on a cabinet door. Her question to me was rather obvious but here it came anyway, "Can you paint scenes on canvases?" Duh, yes (I actually answered her a lot nicer than that but didn't she know that if I can paint on wood, that I can paint on canvas, a wall, a car door, anything she had in mind?). She handed me a couple of photos of paintings that she liked and asked me to paint something along those lines. By the end of the week I had a painting that I delivered to her. She loved it, we agreed to a price, and then she told me she had a summer home in one of the major art communities of Florida and that her sister had a home in Chicago. If I could paint some more paintings like the one she just bought, then she would buy anything and everything I could create. In turn, she and her sister would take the risk of trying to sell them in art galleries in their art communities for a profit. The amount I was paid was less than I would have, should have, or could have sold my paintings for but it was enough to encourage me to paint almost a painting a week for them for almost three years. My "regular" job's work hours at that time were noon until 8:00 so I just got up early, painted for about an hour or two before work and by the end of each week I had a painting that they bought. We did this over and over until I had painted almost 150 paintings of a significant size. In that time I not only learned how to stretch my own canvas to keep my costs down, but somewhere along the lines I developed a style.

If you don't run across that "magic patron" like I did, set yourself up with an imaginary (or real) deadline to finish X number of pieces. Make it a deadline (RAD) that will push you just enough to cross the threshold from hobbyist, working on your art in your "free" time, to professional artist, working on your art as a sort of "job". Make it a challenge not only in numbers but in quality as well. Instead of working and re-working one piece, take an idea that developed as you worked on that piece and make it the beginning of a second or third piece. (RAD) This could also form the basis of a "series"

26

which creates a great show, by the way.

How many pieces will create a style? From a gallery standpoint, I always recommend that for an artist who wants a show, they need to bring me 15 - 20 paintings in a particular style or theme, or 30 or more photographs in a particular style or theme, or 5 - 10 sculpted pieces in a style or theme before I can tell who or what they are as an artist. Pretend that you are working for a show in a major gallery. Set your imaginary deadline with these numbers in mind. Keep in mind that these numbers do NOT mean the total number of pieces you will create, but the total number of pieces that actually are alike style-wise. That means you might actually create twice or three times the desired number before they seem to fall into a style category. But if you can spend this time creating anything you want to create, ultimately, the style will find itself. Just keep working and trust me, before you know it a style is born.

Well, you are saying, "thank you very much for the notification that I've got to work so hard to develop a style but you don't know my time and space limitations". Oh yes, I do. My first studio (if you could call it that) was an unheated, un-air conditioned corner of the garage. I actually had to paint in gloves during the winter (with the fingers cut out so I could grip the brush) with my husband's old overalls over my ski pants and one little space heater that did practically nothing but keep my paint from freezing. In the summer I kept cool by painting in shorts with a water spray bottle and a huge fan that blew garage trash onto my work. So no matter what your

27

"studio" conditions or excuses, I've heard them all from other artists and none of them is an excuse that can't be overcome with a proper space and a little time management in order to work properly. That brings us to the trials and errors, tricks and tips to creating both space and time to work.

Chapter 4/Step 4: Create Space and Time

Space

We're going to assume that you began reading this book because you are serious about selling your art. Just like anything else, when you get serious about something, the things around you change or at least they should change.

One of the things that needs to change in preparation to sell your art is the area in which you create the art. Are you still working at the kitchen table or do you have a "real" studio? Where you work and how you manage your time tells you how serious you take your artwork. And if you don't take your artwork serious, then who will?

When I first began to take my artwork serious, I cleared out a place in the garage to work. Basically it was because the work I was doing at the time was too big for my kitchen table. I had also already ruined the linoleum floor in the kitchen with paint splatters, so for the sake of my home and its' shape, I needed to move out of the house.

Once my oldest son left for college, I immediately took over his room as a "for real" studio with indoor plumbing and everything. By this time I was taking my art career pretty seriously so I painted the walls, installed a large flat table, set up the easel on a new linoleum floor and back into business I went.

Sometimes you luck up and get an empty room to use as you please. Sometimes you build something in the back yard. Sometimes you stay at your kitchen table. But you'll never know what you need in a studio until you "paint, paint, paint", "sculpt, sculpt, sculpt" or "create, create, create". Are you really going to need a flat surface or will most of your work fit on the wall or an easel? If you need a darkroom or storage, how will you handle that? Until you have created a pattern to your work habits you may just go out and buy a bunch of plastic containers for no reason. Or like a friend of mine, spend all your time sorting you "stuff" until there's no time to work. Remember that work is of the essence so just start working and quickly you will see the "must haves" followed by the "could also needs", and finally the "might needs" along with the comfort items or the "would like to haves".

Let's start with the "must haves". Up to now you are working on your artwork anywhere you can (RAD) and as you work you quickly see your "must haves". A comfortable seat plus your workstation, easel, stand(s) and tables are absolute necessities. All of these items must be easily accessible without any prep time needed for set up. In other words, you should never have to clear off dishes to work or move any of your "must haves" other than in preparation for the artwork itself. Any excess "work" to get to your art space can deter even the most inspired muse. As you work (RAD) you'll also begin to see what items you don't need to have

30

immediately at hand or items that you don't use as often as you thought you might use. As you work, group the "must have" items until you actually see how much space is needed for each group. Now you can start to visualize what containers and in particular how many and what size containers you will need. Before you run out to buy a bunch of stuff, look around your home for creative containers (after all, you ARE and artist). (RAD)

For lighting, if you are lucky enough to have north light available then your lighting battle is half over. If you have a choice in rooms or spaces in your home (both kids just moved out) then pick the one with the best light. No light or very little light? These problems can be overcome easily and not necessarily expensively. There are certain things you will need to scrimp on when it comes to your studio, certain things you can re-purpose but lighting is a must in the "best that you can afford" category. Now, I'm not saying that I haven't created some of my best work in bad light situations, but for the sake of your eyes and so that there are no surprises when you take that piece out to the show or when you need to photograph it, you need to get the best lighting available for your work with whatever budget you have.

For the set up of the studio let me take you on a mini tour of my work space. In my studio, I paint in oil so to the right of my easel is an old jewelry stand with drawers for each color of paint (categorized by reds, blues, greens, etc). My large brushes are standing with the brush up in a plastic bin from an art shop that went out of business and my small

31

brushes are standing with the   brush up in an old ice cream bucket.   Linseed oil and mineral spirits are in their own large containers on the floor. For lighting I have a sliding glass door facing north and a daylight lamp but I started out with a shop light and desk lamps so use what you have until you can provide exactly what you need.   With just the easel, a chair, and place to put my paint,   all I have to do is put a canvas on the easel and start painting.   I could paint forever with just this set up so if I had to limit my space, these would be the things I would put out and I could plan accordingly.   These first "must haves" for your work should determine the minimum amount of space needed for your work area. Once you know this you may be surprised how well that small space under the stairs or that extra closet might suit you or you may find it's time to start looking at that old garage or empty guest house with a different eye.

   With all of your "must haves" in place you can begin working on your artwork at a moment's notice. (RAD) As you work, now,   you'll start finding room for the "could also needs". If there is no room in your workspace, try to find a nearby space or closet.   Think "up" and you may find some unused shelf space.   Think "down" and you might find an empty space under a bed, couch or counter. Mainly, I work in oil but I also teach classes in acrylics (my "could also needs") so I have a rack for acrylic paints, buckets for water and sponges and stamps for texture along with my spackle and varnish which I put under the "table" in my first studio. This "table" was the old family pool table that I covered with a large
32

sturdy board.   It made not only a great work and storage station but if the family wanted to dust off the pool balls and play a game, the top was easily moved.   In my current studio, (which was once the family "gym") these paints are out of the way in a file cabinet which easily rolls close to my easel when I switch mediums.

Another important part of my "could also needs" is my collection of books and reference materials. These can easily be located   completely outside my work area.   In fact, they seem to be even more convenient to me in the family library where I can read in quiet (RAD) or next to my chair in the den where I can leaf through art magazines in the evenings while I watch TV.   Art magazines are my weakness so I try to keep only one magazine rack full of art magazines.   I make myself tear out the articles and pictures I think I will need once a new magazine comes into the house and store these for reference in a nearby file cabinet.   I share the rest of the magazine with my art students and fellow artists and they do likewise. The file cabinet becomes my "idea cabinet".   If you are super organized you can actually put files in the cabinet with labels as to things like "trees",   "business ideas" or "people", "places", and "things".   Then you can rip out all the pages of the magazines that have been accumulating and file photos or articles for reference in your work.   You can even, dare I say, rip up the art books, too.   As for me, I just pile the pictures and articles in the cabinet with no rhyme or reason.   I actually enjoy the process of flipping through everything when I need a break and letting the ideas come from whatever I happen to come upon.

. And speaking of space how's the storage in your space? Storage areas are perfect for the "might needs" like framing tools, screwdrivers, wire, packing materials, etc. In addition to looking high and low for this space make use of boxes and baskets wherever you can but always try to either label what is in the boxes or use clear containers so that you can see all of your stuff. Out of site means out of mind and there's nothing worse than wasting money buying something you already have three or four of because you couldn't find the first one.

Finally you can address the "would like to haves". How about some creature comforts, too? Can you work to music or while watching TV? If so, and if there's room available, add a radio or TV to your studio. Remember to look high and low for places to get them in there but try to put them out of your way like using wall mount TVs and locating stereos in the other room, running wires to the speaker cabinets that can serve double duty as pedestals in your studio. Do certain pictures or scenes inspire you? Hang pictures or pin inspirational items to a cork board. Don't forget a calendar and a few business items.

Business items? Oh no, here we go opening that can of worms. We'll talk more about what you actually need to do to make this a viable business later but for now suffice it to say that you do need a clear desk space or portion of a desk for your business items, a separate set of drawers or files, and a comfortable chair with good light away from areas of paint splatters, chemicals or dust. If this needs to be in another room

34

or if you already have a home office, then your business could probably be better done next to or near your computer area.

By now, if you've been practicing RAD (reading, assimilating and doing) you should have the beginnings of a good working studio. You no longer have to clear off the kitchen table or drag your paints or wood working tools out of a closet. You have a space to go to at a moments notice and you have eliminated the excuse of having no space to work. Now you need to create some time to work.

Time

There are only 24 hours in a day, 7 days in a week, and 52 weeks to a year but you can make this time work to your benefit once you have your space set up and start adhering to a little discipline with your time. I hate to even use the work "discipline" because it may be a word connected or associated with "pain" to you – Au contraire!

The best way to get time on your side is to understand how time really affects you. Instead of trying to "make" time for art, let it become a natural part of your day. This way you'll begin to manage your time instead of your time managing you. Here's how to make that happen.

Begin your time management right now with a brief daily journal. (RAD) Begin in the morning and note the time of day that you feel the most productive. You may already know the answer to this, but if you don't, begin your journal by jotting down all the big blocks of times and what you do with that time   for at least one week (a normal week, not a vacation week). After a week you should be able to see some sort of daily pattern emerge. This pattern will at least tell you if you are a morning person or more productive in the afternoon or maybe even a late night productive person.   Watch how your daily chore schedule fits into this plan or if you work outside your home and are on someone else's time clock, completely block out that section of time and essentially pretend that it doesn't exist. The only time you may have to even think about art when you are on someone else's time clock is maybe your lunch time that might afford you a quick trip to the mall for a tube of paint or a 10-15 min break to read a new art article. Maybe right now, your job (the one that is currently paying the bills) must come first.   It's understandable and it's a fact of life.   But what are you doing with the rest of the day, and how about the weekends?   How much of it is spent actually productive and how much is not?   Once you have established a time journal for what you are doing right now, I'm still not going to ask you to make any changes . . . yet.

Take the journal and categorize the time as "needs" and "wants".   Was that time spent doing something you actually "need" to do like grocery shopping or something you "want" to do like watch TV? (RAD)

The time that you have for "needs" and "wants" must now be critically assessed.   First of all, is it a real need or just something you feel like you have to do and that's the only time that you can do it. Do you see where you may be   taking too much time with wasted activities?   Remember, you have decided to become a professional artist and just like taking on a new job, there must be time to fit this activity into your schedule.

Let me stress the importance of your time management with these stories:

Early in my art career I was an art teacher. I taught at the junior high level so basically I was a "babysitter" for my students during the years when their hormones really kicked in. Teaching art at the junior high level was particularly stressful because I honestly tried to teach and to adhere to all the school guidelines, recommendations, rules and beaurocratic nonsense. By the time the summer rolled around (and I told myself this all year) I figured that I would work on my art then. During the school year I had spent all day trying to keep students from slinging paint, making tattoos with India ink and such so coming home in the afternoon to work on my own art was out of the question. I was just too burnt out. The last thing I wanted to see was a paintbrush. Once the summer came around I was all "gung ho" to create my own art and really begin to break into the professional venue of artists. But for the first week or so I really just needed to rest. Then I began to meet up with friends for lunch since I couldn't take nice lunch breaks during the school year. Then came vacation which I owed myself big time and "oh no, what's this? School starts next week? I've got to make some plans and . . ." well, you see what I mean. Having a summer blocked off to accomplish my goal was too broad a time frame and too many distractions got in the way. I did this for almost 10 years before I finally realized it would never work and I would have to try something else.

I've found that the "something else" was this. I needed to try to make the time for artistic self improvement something I would look forward to rather than something I felt I needed to do. I already had plenty of things I "needed" to do. Art had to be something I wanted to do so that I could keep the passion alive.

Once I bit the bullet and quit teaching, my new job hours became something more manageable with my life and personal work style. This new job required hours of about noon until about 8 pm   The best thing about the noon start time was that I found that I was a morning person and was able to create a schedule whereby I got up about 6:30 or 7:00 each morning, got showered and cooked breakfast, read the paper, washed the dishes and straightened up the kitchen, put in a load of laundry and painted for about an hour. Now, my space was already set up as yours should be by now (RAD) and the paint was there waiting for me.   There was no wasted time or "work" to getting all my art stuff out before I started to paint. All I did was put on a smock over my jammies and sit down at the easel.   Just like clockwork I continued working on a piece from the past day or began a new piece. If I really needed the muse to be on my shoulder I might read an inspirational art book or art magazine article before I began.   Canvas was readily available or paper on which to sketch and it was all within easy reach.   Now, the time I worked at my art might have   only been about an hour per day but just like exercising

38

as long as I made it a regular part of my day, then it showed benefits. I also had motivation.

Motivation and time management go hand in hand. This was that time in my life when I had met a lady who loved my work, believed in me and was buying everything I could create. I would usually have a complete painting done by Friday of each week and I delivered it to her on my way to work. I got paid upon delivery. It's amazing how payment can motivate a person. But even if you don't have a "for real" motivation like immediate payment or a show to work towards, then try making an imaginary one for yourself. Tell yourself that if you get X number of pieces of art (or a part of a piece of art) done by X time, then you get X reward. Set up these dates and times on your calendar. Push yourself just a little. Reward yourself. Be your own art patron.

Back to your time journal, (RAD) once you've taken a good look, you might just see a block of an hour or so that really is either being wasted or needs to be refocused into your new career. It would be best if it was the same time every day so that a habit could more easily be formed but whatever time you have, take a big red pen and write over that time "Art Career"(RAD) and use it as such.

In the beginning if you are still creating a "style" you'll need this time to just paint or create. Later on, this time can be divided into business time, inspiration time, and creation time. But for now just make sure it is some sort of "art time".

So you now have a space, some time, a deadline, either

39

real or imaginary, and you're still not getting those creative juices flowing. When you enter your art space all you do is stare at the canvas or clay or camera or whatever medium is available. I saw a quote the other day that said "Inspiration is for amateurs, the rest of us just get to work." If you have to, use this as your mantra to get yourself in gear. If you find that you really need to get inspired first, though, there are lots of ways to "kick start" your muse. At the very least read something motivational or art related. When nothing seems to come to you just slap some paint on the canvas or try a new subject matter or style, take photos of your home or studio. Remember, it's only paint, or clay, or canvas, or film. You can rework it if it is not successful. Don't be too concerned that every work of art has to have a successful completion or be a masterpiece.

Here's a fun way to motivate yourself that I often use. I found a book titled <u>Water Color Bold and Free</u> by Lawrence Goldsmith. I don't even do watercolors much anymore (see, you can get ideas from outside your "box") but I liked the book in particular because each page listed an experiment to do with watercolors. I took each experiment, like the instructions for a project titled "Gray Field with Bright Accents" or "Let a Motif Stand Alone" and wrote them on a piece of paper. There are over 60 experiments in this book. You can use the same ones or perhaps use ideas from other books, classes or articles. Keep a small notebook handy next to your "inspiration chair" and jot down ideas that come to you from movies or from everyday life. Write these ideas on slips of paper and put them
40

in a box or bag. Pick one at random to inspire experimentation. (RAD) Again, not every piece has to be a completed, great, historically significant, successful work of art and the more you create, the more your style will come into play, the more inspiration and motivation you will have, and the more time you'll spend on your art career leading to more sales which leads to more inspiration and motivation which leads to more creativity which leads to more. . . well, you get the picture. It's all starting to work fabulously if you are still practicing your RAD and more and more, better and better, pieces are being created. Now that didn't hurt, did it?

Chapter 5/Step 5: Build a Body of Work

Now that you are working in an appropriate studio with time on your side, you should start to see an accumulation of artwork beginning to surround you. Some of it is very good and some of it is not so good. Some of it is merely sketches or ideas.

In the beginning, you'll probably see a hodge podge of themes, subject matter, color schemes or mediums. That's fine, just keep working. The most important thing is to create. Even if nothing you do seems to relate to anything else you have already done, just continue to work.

Make it fun, though. Work on what your muse leads you to work on. Experiment anyway you desire. Do fast work, do slow work, do detailed work, do free hand work, but do some artwork.

As your   artwork begins to accumulate, start some sort of categorizing system. (RAD) Stack all the photos of trees in one pile, the paintings of people in another, the cups and saucers in clay on a shelf separate from the bowls and pitchers. Then notice which pile is biggest, or which pile is your favorite, or which pile is just junk. Yep, you'll probably have a pile of that, too.

But as you look at the "piles" you'll be amazed as something starts to "click" inside of you telling you that you're on the right track. It's either the passion for what you created or the pat on the back that you give yourself when you actually tell yourself, "hey, that's pretty darn good".

You may even find that, with your "favorite" piles you are able to explain why it is important to you, and as you explain it to yourself and others you begin to create a professional "voice" for your artwork. You may see your passion stirred up to create only this theme or medium or style and that's the point that we are working toward. In creating a specific amount of work, you are creating your body of work. It is this body of work with which you will start your sales career. These will be the pieces that you can proudly offer to the public knowing that as they sell, there is more inside of you where this first body of work came from. I'm not saying that you won't stray every now and then toward an experiment or two in your artwork (which could ultimately still be used in your body of work or create a whole new body of work) but you now have a focus and direction for your artwork. This is not only your style but also your passion and it's what makes it more "art" and less "work". There's a lot less experimentation and struggle and a lot more creating with a professional attitude.

So how many pieces makes up a good body of work?

From the aspect of sales a good body of work needs to be   approximately 20–30 paintings or 50-75 photos or 5-10 sculptures in one obvious style.   As a gallery owner I would feel safe having a show with an artist who had this many available pieces from which I could select   and offer to my customers.   Even if you are selling directly to the public, this gives you enough pieces to select your best "show" pieces and to have plenty of work to offer your customers.   Viewers will know exactly who you are as an artist and because you understand more about why these pieces were created, you will be able to articulate where they came from and how you came to this point in your professionalism.

Congratulations.   You now have a style, a passion for what you are doing; you have the time to do it, the skill and the space.   This is the body of work with which you will begin your professional artist sales career.

Your body of work now says "I am a portrait artist" or "I paint landscapes" or "I photograph bridges in black and white".   As a gallery owner or customer, I'm going to recognize you and your talent more immediately than I would had you spent two to three hours of my time vaguely trying to tell me who you are and what you do and showing me a ton of work that's all over the place.

You are also   creating a name for yourself.   To begin with it may   be more like "the artist who paints those great sunsets" or the "hat guy" who photographs people in hats or the "leaf lady" who does leaf sculptures or fine pencil sketches

44

of leaves.   But soon it will be "Joe Smith who does the hat photos" or "Mary Jones who accents her sunsets with that fabulous violet color".   Then it won't be long before it's "That's a Joe Smith original", or "I'm a collector of   Mary Jones work".

Now that you have your style in a body of work, where do you go from here?

Chapter 6/Step 6: Reach Your Destination

Now we get to the "nitty gritty" of the marketing process, the ultimate goal for our marketing and the destination that all roads lead to. I'm talking about "selling" your art. In the following chapters we will be setting destinations for selling your art. I call them destinations because just like a road map, you'll be following a path to where you want to be in the selling of your art. If you start off down the road for selling your art and don't know where you are going then everything you have done up to now could be in vain.

To find your destination you need to figure out just what you really want from the sale of your artwork. Now before you scream out that you want to be rich and famous, start looking at your lifestyle and let's talk about the different stages or destinations that lead to the possibility of your "rich and famous" goal.

I've divided your art destinations into five "locations" that, with serious assessment of your lifestyle, may suit you even better than the "rich and famous" goal or at least make you comfortable on your way to this goal. Between the five

46

locations you may even be able to create your own personal destination or goal for which you want to strive. Each location

is not necessarily less or greater, better or worse, than the others. Each location is a place in which you may pause, stop, "vacation" or spend a comfortable lifetime. And if you choose a location that at any time doesn't feel right anymore, then you can feel free to reevaluate that location, get out your "roadmap" or mental GPS and head to a new destination. None of the locations has to be taken in order either but reading through the details of each location will help teach   you to become more profitable. Once you learn what is required to reach each location you can choose to stop there,   continue on, or change directions as your muse and pocketbook dictate.

I give you these locations in what I feel are the simplest to the most complicated due to the specific challenges involved to get there.   As you see the descriptions, you'll understand more fully.   And even if you feel like skipping a   destination or two,   I highly recommend that you at least read through the information for other "locations" for there is a wealth of information to be gleaned from each and you will gain a greater appreciation for your fellow artists and their chosen locations as you learn more about the specifics.

Location one, and perhaps the easiest location to reach is HOBBY town. At this location you've picked up some art tools, whether they were your child's left over school art supplies or the art supplies you found from your collage classes or maybe something you found on sale and always wanted to try out. The investment is minimal and there's absolutely no pressure to create something "grand". It makes you feel good to create the artwork and that's ultimately the only goal you need to have to live in HOBBY town. It's a wonderful location and many good things can come about from this work done as a hobbyist.

One artist friend of mine literally "found" some paints and brushes on the side of the road, began to paint for fun and is now a well known local artist who moved from painting on cardboard to canvas. Another artist friend of mine found that she couldn't sleep well at night so she began to paint to pass the long night hours. An interior decorator saw her work and the rest was history. Still another artist friend found that painting seemed to ease her migraines. People loved her abstract creations and again, the rest is history. All three artists were creating more or less as a hobby, just for fun, and before they knew it they had a body of work that was recognized. That's the best case scenario if you are looking to sell, but as a hobbyist, just the sheer joy of creation is the ultimate and most satisfactory goal, sales or no sales. There is no pressure to create and the act of creating is the end in itself.

The business details of being a hobbyist consist of keeping up with all receipts for supplies if for no other reason than to see if you are breaking even, making a profit, or just enjoying an expensive hobby. That's all you have to do but if you want or need to get your supplies wholesale, you'll need a

48

business license and/or tax number. For this you need to contact your local small business bureau. They'll be happy to help. You also want to keep the receipts in case you need or want to file your taxes with your supplies as deductions. The IRS says that after three years, if you have not made a profit on your artwork, then it is to be considered a hobby, anyway, but if and when the money starts rolling in and your hobby does start to become profitable, it may be advantageous to list yourself as an artist on your tax return and deduct supply costs and expenses. If this happens you should already be in the habit of at least "shoe box organization" of your expenses.

A special note here – I will not even pretend to be an expert on all tax or business laws for your state, community or the IRS. Get some expert advice on these matters, often found for free through seminars or available at your local library or small business office.

I call location two the land of RETURN ON YOUR INVESTMENT. This land could naturally follow the path from HOBBY town especially if the hobby is "getting out of hand".

A fiber artist that I know loved to knit scarves. Just her spare time activity of creating beautiful scarves was the satisfaction in itself but soon she found herself with way too many scarves. She'd given plenty to friends and family and though they loved her work, they had all the scarves they needed. Still she had the desire to make more but found herself with   a shortage of funds to buy more yarn.   Thus her hobby led to a desire to have a return on her investment. Setting her scarves up in local gift and clothing stores gave her enough money to buy more yarn to create more scarves. Making a profit on the scarves was not the issue.   She just had the time and desires to create more scarves and all she needed was to get enough money from each scarf to create one or more new scarves. Since profit was not much of a consideration this was a lovely way for her to work but if you work this way   I ask you to please be considerate of those who need to make a profit from their artwork.

Consider it this way: Your neighbor artist at the crafts fair has three kids to feed so she tries to sell her scarves for $45 each and you know that you can sell a comparable scarf at $20 and "break even".   That may be great for your sales but you've ruined an opportunity for someone who really needs to make a profit.

Plus, maybe that scarf you created only took $5 of yarn and 3 hours to make BUT how about the expense of the booth or the shop commission, the cost of the packaging for the scarf and the containers to transport them, the value of the time it took to design and create the sales tags plus the value of the time and gas it took you took to travel to and sit all weekend at the crafts fair.   Before you say that the return on your investment is just the cost of the yarn, consider all the true expenses and figure out your "bottom line".   We'll cover more details, tips and tricks about getting your "bottom line" in chapter 8.

50

For business purposes as an artist that is trying to make a RETURN ON YOUR INVESTMENT, you may find that if you are not re-cooping the cost of your supplies, then   you are really just wasting your time, financially, so you better be enjoying that time a lot. Keep receipts like you would as a hobbyist and then figure out if there needs to be a change due to the need to make more money or if you're just "paying to play".   There's nothing right or wrong with your decision. If you want to "pay to play" then that's fine.   It just needs to feel right for you.

That brings us to location three – the beautiful tropical island of FUN MONEY.   What I'm talking about here is NOT money that you have to have to put food on the table. Fun money means that once you sell your artwork, you have money not only for paying your expenses but you also have some for buying more supplies (reinvesting in your work), paying whatever bills are necessary to be paid with your profits AND you have some extra money above and beyond. With this money there are no bills you have to cover so you   can take your wife out to dinner to make up for all the hours you spent in the wood shed carving wooden figurines or you can treat yourself and the family to a weekend camping trip or maybe it's even enough to send yourself back to art school. With a definite monetary goal in mind, you can actually project how many figurines or scarves or paintings you would need to sell to pay for a trip to Europe or build a new studio.

There's even a way to get "free" stuff as a profit for

your artwork. I went to a workshop with watercolorist Tom Lynch years ago and he told us of doing workshops on cruise ships in return for a free cruise for himself and his family. All he had to do was lead a two hour workshop a few times during the week long cruise. How about trading your artwork for a week at your friend's lakeside cabin? As an artist, I've even swapped painting for painting with another artist whose work I admired but couldn't afford. When I found out the feeling was mutual, we made an awesome swap.

This is a delightful stage to be in whether by chance or by purposeful work and calculation. But if your artwork starts making more money than you can have fun with or reinvest, then you may be getting the attention of the IRS. Galleries and even craft shows are often required to submit your total sales amounts to the government or a corporate client may have deducted the price of your sculpture on their tax return, thereby informing the IRS that you are a viable "business". For all moral and legal obligations, you will need to keep records so that the profit margin can be accurately reported, deductions can be made, and everyone will get their fair share. No matter what destination you reach in your artwork it's always a good idea to keep all of your receipts. (Seems like I've said that before – it must be important. RAD) Even if you never use them for business purposes, years later you may enjoy looking back on them and laughing at how "cheap" those expensive art supplies used to be when you were a struggling "starving" artist.

That brings us to the next location in your chosen art career, the city of SOME PROFIT. At this location you have a definite need either because artwork is your major source of income or a much needed secondary income and/or an important supplement to your financial lifestyle. Once you have paid for your art supplies, you have a need, not just a desire, to make some sort of overall profit. To raise the profit level you may need to find wholesale suppliers or find a way to cut corners on the expense of the creation of your pieces. I learned to stretch canvas for my paintings in collage and that knowledge alone was worth the seven years I invested in my Bachelors and Master's degree programs. I can create a canvas for about 1/10th of what I would spend in the art supply stores or even online. Repurposing is also useful to increase your profit margin. I've painted over many a canvas and the results were beautiful.

There is no doubt that at this point you will need to keep up with all paperwork, file taxes, get business licenses and wholesale numbers. Any small business group or organization in your town will tell you what you need and how to get the correct forms. Don't be afraid of being taxed as an artist. Just as you do with your personal taxes, be honest and back up everything you put down in writing and you'll be fine.

At this stage, your artwork becomes more like your "job" but it's still the best job to have. And it's all going to be contingent upon how important it is to "put food on the table" so to speak. You may find yourself creating toward what will sell more than creating for your own personal enjoyment. If

53

this just grates against your soul, consider creating one or two items to sell and then creating one for your own enjoyment. Maybe you can paint portraits to put food on the table but create at least one abstract painting a week to release your artistic muse. The ideal situation is when you create what you love and that makes the money for you but if that isn't happening you have two choices. You can create what sells and make up for your frustration by rewarding yourself in other ways like I've just mentions or by doing things like taking a nice vacation every time you reach a monetary goal or you can always go back to that corporate or blue collar 9 – 5 job and paint in your spare time as a hobby. You make the tough decision here.

Sadly, at this stage I've seen many a fabulous extremely talented artist forced into a "day job" to support their art career. If this is you, just remember our first step to selling and never say less than "I'm an artist currently working as a _____" and keep on creating. In the years to come no one may remember that you were a _____ but your artwork may speak volumes about who you really were.

Finally and ultimately there's the location and destination of being a TOTAL PROFESSIONAL. This is a point where your artwork is your major source of income. You have no other means whereby you make the mortgage payments and bills and contrary to popular belief, it is an accessible goal. It just depends on how hard you work and how much you are willing to sacrifice to get to this point. Making a living doing what your passion dictates, is a wonderful way to live. It's not always easy and you may have to deviate just a little from your ideal vision of life at this stage but you can make it. And again, it's going to depend on how badly you need to put food on the table as to how much deviation you may need to make. I know of many artists who have been known to paint commissions that they weren't exactly inspired to do, or photograph an event that they weren't really interested in, but they are making their living through their artwork and that is the important thing.

On the business side of being a TOTAL PROFESSIONAL you must keep up with all paperwork, schedule your time and efforts, and direct yourself to what is most productive to your monetary success. Paperwork can be kept any way from "shoebox style" to computer generated programs but it MUST be kept current. Your time may have to be divided into segments to get all the "work" done. You may need to work an entire day or two on business paperwork or promotion leaving only three to four days for actual creativity. All of your conversations, relationships, and even your "time off" may center on your art career but if you love what you do it will just come naturally.

As a final note on this and on any destination that you choose, I give you the story of an artist named Jimmy. When I was going to art school I bought my art supplies from the local art store where Jimmy worked. Little did I know that Jimmy was also an artist who excelled in painting extreme realism. Jimmy had dropped out of art school because, at that time, extreme realism was not in vogue and he went in search of an art school that would teach him what he desired most – to learn more about the old masters and their use of paint and light. He found such a school in Italy, of all places, but his meager income and the fact that he came from a poor home with a single mom raising him and his siblings made the dream of attending such a school seem impossible. Art school had been paid for with a scholarship but if it wasn't where he wanted to be then there was no sense wasting his time.

Instead, Jimmy contacted the teacher of the Italian school and told him that he was coming to classes. The teacher responded with "Great, when can I sign you up?" Jimmy's answer was "You don't understand. I don't have the money now but I'm coming. It may not be this year or next year or even the year after, but I'm coming". With that determination in mind, Jimmy shared a small apartment with his brother, saving almost every penny of every paycheck until he had not only enough money for the school but he also had enough money for living expenses for the duration his education. As Jimmy put it, he was going to devote himself completely to studying art without worrying about getting a job or where his next meal was coming from or anything but the study and creation of his art.

Sure enough, seven years later, Jimmy left for Italy and a one and one half year course turned into 14 years of living in Italy, studying the great masters. All the while Jimmy's work grew to a fantastic level of skill and once the New York galleries began visiting his little studio, the rest became history.

Jimmy is now a TOTAL PROFESSIONAL making all of his bills and more from the 5 and 6 figure sale prices of his work.

Whichever location, whichever destination you select as a good one to work toward or whichever location or destination you happen to "fall into" as you market your art, you'll never have to whine and cry about your art career. You'll be too busy working on your art and its' marketing. And as the movie said "If you build it they will come," with proper direction, focus, and determination, "If you create it, you will be successful."

Chapter7/Step 7: RAD the Tips and Tricks

Whenever I teach my marketing workshops and classes, one of the first things we do is introduce ourselves around the room and tell each other a little about ourselves. As I've told you before, one of the reasons is to see how many people actually call themselves an "artist." Another reason I find this useful is as one of the first steps to finding places to sell – to network market yourself. Nine times out of ten, there will be someone in that workshop or class who has access to something you need to know, or connections with someone who knows someone who knows someone who will advance your chosen career. Keep this networking idea in mind with everything you do in art whether it's a meeting of other artists, a social gathering, membership in an organization or a show. It's the new way of doing business and irregardless of how much you advertise or sit at your computer making "cold calls" to galleries or stores, knowing someone who knows someone can be worth its' weight in gold. Not very social? Just be your artistic self ("I am an artist") and let the conversation flow everywhere you go. That's networking in a nutshell. And networking is a huge "trick" for selling your artwork.

58

In the last chapter we talked about the destinations that you might take in your art career. You may have found that one destination sounds more or less attractive and fitting for your artwork than another. Likewise you will find that there are "tips and tricks" (ways and places) to sell your particular artwork that may appeal to you more than others. And you never know where you may end up in your efforts to become a successful marketing artist. So just as you have chosen the destination or location that seems to "fit" likewise you will be choosing the ways and places or as I call them, the creative "tips and tricks" that work best for selling your artwork. Watch for what not only "fits" your career goal and destination but what also "feels" right to you as you RAD.

CRAFT/ART SHOWS

One of the first and easiest ways to get you artwork out there is through CRAFT OR ART SHOWS. There is a big difference between the two. If you have more crafty items you will gear your sales toward the craft shows but if your art is more along the lines of fine art, then you will need to concentrate on the more fine art/art shows. The initial difference can be as simple as cost or application process. To find the best "fit" for your artwork sales there are a couple of "tips and tricks" to learn.

Visiting the art/craft shows is the best tip to finding out if this "show" is for you and your artwork. (RAD) First of all, it is really fun to "have" to go the all the local and out of town shows. I once worked for a huge craft design company which required me to visit shops and galleries and arts and crafts shows to see the latest in arts and craft trends. It was a "tough" job but somebody had to do it. Seriously, though, if you want to really find out if this is a good show you not only need to attend but you need to make note of the show's visitors. As you walk around a show do you see visitors eating, talking, and socializing or walking around with sacks of items they have bought? Another good trick is to look at the expressions on the faces of the vendors. Are they excited or bored? Do they pack up early? If you get a chance to start up a conversation with them, do they enthusiastically tell you about this show and/or others that they have found productive? Or do they actually "bad-mouth" the venue? Please do not try to take up their valuable customer time or get them to answer these questions if they seem hesitant, but once in a while you'll get a crafter or artist who needs to "spill the beans" and they will tell you all that you need to know and more.

Another good tip for finding good art and craft shows and/or if you can't actually visit the show is through a magazine directed to your particular art or craft. They will list shows in their advertisements (remember that it is an advertisement, not an accurate review) and often have articles submitted by artists who will relate their experiences about a particular show. A really good, non objective listing of shows is through a magazine called Sunshine Arts or Professional Artist Magazine. Sunshine Arts not only gives

60

you excellent advise about selling your art but in the back of the magazine it lists shows that occur seasonally, where they are, the requirements to get in the show (the stricter they are, the more fine art or fine craft they may show), how much it costs, deadlines for entries, anything special about the show (like contests and requirements for admission and possible prizes) and most importantly, how many artists return to the show from the previous year. Knowing the number of return artists is the most beneficial information to successful selling because if an artist is doing well at a show, they will come back to that show. If the show has a high rate of return artists, then you would assume that those artists liked the show. Artists usually like the show because they are making a profit from the show. And that makes this show a good one to check out.

Once you have found the shows that you want to try, you've just touched the tip of the iceberg in actually getting there. Getting that first show under your belt, however, makes the next show and the show after that a whole lot easier. But to get that first show you will definitely have, at least, an application to fill out and a fee to pay. It could be as simple as name and address, what you sell, and where you need to send the booth rent check and by what date. Do not miss the deadline or you will either be turned down or you will get the "worst" spot at the show. Sometimes just because you are a "first timer" to the show you'll get a pretty "bad" spot. If you've got confidence, a good product and an attractive display, though, you can still be successful no matter where they "stick" you and your booth.

Next, as my husband calls them, there are always those "but first I gotta" things to do before you can get to the real activity. For instance, when you need to get the weeds cut down around the flower bed, first you have to oil up and load string to the weed eater, but in our case, we're out of string, so we have to go to the store to find the correct string, come home and re-string the weed eater (always a "fun" chore) plus find the extension cord before we can get to the actual chore of cutting the weeds.

In the case of the arts and crafts show, you'll have a lot of these "but first I gotta" things. Like for example, if you choose to use electricity (which will usually cost more on the application), you'll need your own extension cords and from personal experience, you may need a huge length of cord. I once had to set up in the very middle of a huge gym meaning my cord had to be almost 100' long. In addition, to keep the traffic from tripping over the cord, you will need duct tape to tape the cord down to the floor all the way across to your booth. Even if the show has put you right next to the receptacle, you may find that three other people need to use that one receptacle so that someone has to have an adaptor or plug in strip. As far as tables go, if you rent them from the show, you can almost be guaranteed that they are either really old or really heavy. Likewise if you provide your own tables, do you have a vehicle big enough to transport them and all your artwork? All of these things are the "but first I gotta have" items before you even begin to pack the artwork.

62

Once the electricity is provided and the tables are set up, what will be the overall look to your space? The best way to decide on the look of your space is to map off at home, an equal space to what you are renting. (RAD) Most spaces come in 10 X 10 or 12 X 12 blocks. Mark something the correct size out on the floor of the garage or den, someplace that has plenty of room to walk around.   Is the space going to have a back wall to it or will you be out in the center of a big warehouse?   Lots of times you won't know this until you get there so how will you handle items that need to be hung when there is no wall on which to hang them?

Within your marked space, figure out where everything will go. (RAD) Use ideas from all those shows you visited. Notice how the artists put things together and how difficult or easy they have made it for themselves.   When I set up, I used my own tables which were several 2' X 4' tables rather than anything larger.   I could carry two of these at a time without any help. Even though my husband often helped me with set up and take down, there were shows he couldn't attend and I had to set up everything myself.   Make yourself as self-sufficient as possible and when help arrives, you'll have it made.

Next, you'll need to think about the attractiveness of your booth.   I bought cheap plastic table coverings from the local party supply store (they come in all colors but try to pick colors that won't clash with your artwork). Because they are inexpensive, you can use them a couple of times and then just replace them so they always look new. I have seen, however, depending on your artwork or craft, some clever table cover ideas like old quilts or antique tablecloths. Just be ready for customers who want to buy the table covering and not your art if you get too clever.

For the back wall, you can create a pipe and drape from actual pipe and draperies (check the yellow pages for store supplies or go to StoreSupply.com for a good selection) or create your own from pvc pipes and fittings. If you are setting up outdoors you will need weights to hold these pipes down in case of high winds. Also outdoors you'll need a tent which can be purchased almost anywhere these days. Make sure you have help even if it's labeled "easy to install". Art supply magazines have really fancy, made-for-shows, tents with places for signs and "lockable" sides for when you have to leave your booth overnight. Other tents can just be roofs only (if you only need to brave the sun) or they may have full enclosures like beach huts.   If you have one of these, sometimes there is a way that you can use the back and side flaps as a back and side wall but you have to put very light weight items on them.

I also recommend a metal grid system for display (again, the best I have found was through StoreSupply.com). I purchased several panels and found that if I set up so that the panels were at angles to each other, that I could actually connect them with plastic zip tie straps which I simply cut off at the end of the show.   A bag of these was easy to use and inexpensive to buy versus the actual metal connectors. Once

64

you check out the Store Supply catalogue or another store supply company's merchandise you'll see all sorts of shelving and hooks and signage display items which will give you tons of set-up ideas.

Another mandatory piece of equipment to your booth is a chair. As you stroll through arts and crafts shows you'll see that the people really making the sales are the ones who are up on their feet talking to the customers. So why do I say you need a chair? Do one craft show and you'll find out why. Once you finish setting up for the day, you'll need to get off your feet for a while, not to mention "down times" when you need a rest. Unless you have help, there is no getting out of the booth except in emergencies (like bathroom trips) so be prepared to sit down at least a little. But don't just get any old lawn chair. If you sit lower than the customer, it puts you in an awkward position to talk unless the chair is chosen because you are actually working and/or demonstrating your artwork. It also makes you look lazy (along with the fact that you may not be able to resist sitting back and munching on nachos the entire day). I recommend a taller stool or director's chair (with a back to it). With one of these I can just about sit down all day. I'm eye level with the customers without having to stand up for each and every one. Once I've "qualified" a customer (more on that in chapter 8) I can jump down and show them around personally.

Back to the space you marked off at home, arrange your chair, tables, easels, grids, and back wall. If the festival is outdoors, practice setting up the tent and actually arranging the booth outdoors. (Some applications for shows even require a picture of your set up, so as long as you are going to all this trouble, have a camera handy for the final look.) As you arrange each item think in terms of the customer. Make sure the customer has easy access to each item, that your set up is secure so that there won't be any accidental breakage or worse yet, customers tripping over anything. Also, make sure you can keep an eye on all your expensive items at all times even when you are making a sale, packing an item, or talking to a customer. This may necessitate lockable cabinets. (Customers hate them and they are a real hassle in a crowd but if the artwork dictates the need, do not hesitate to use them).

Next, put out the artwork. Try using lifts (as simple as empty boxes under the table covering) mini easels, or shelving to make your work standout. Load baskets or bins with less expensive pieces. Put flowers in vases (expect someone to want to buy them). Put food (not the kind that would spoil) on plates to show the plate's purpose.

Once in place, make sure each piece is easily tagged or clearly signed with prices. Make the signs as professional as you can. With computer printers there is really no excuse for hastily written scribbled prices or titles. Depending on your "craft" don't forget to have a variety of prices. Think of creating something that everyone can take home. If they love the expensive item but can't afford it, have smaller prints or similar copies. Always try to have one huge focal point that may be your eye-catcher. This could be the piece that has a price that would "make your day" if it sold, but it also stops customers in their tracks and makes them interested in seeing more of your work.   If you have literally hundreds of your products, make an attractive display with a smaller number of pieces and store the rest under the skirt of the table to replenish as needed.   If you   run out of room, put out your best pieces and be ready to show interested customers a lesser piece that they might be interested in.

A catchy sign   with a catchy name for your product/booth helps people find and remember you.   Often the name of the booth is listed on a roster for the customers as they enter.   If you have a business license, you may have already created your name.   If not, you can make yours as simple as "Portraits by Diane" or more cute-sy like "Puppy Pals" (which really doesn't say what your product is, but it may get you every customer interested in puppies).   Try to repeat this name on all signage.   Make your sign fit your booth.   How about a wood carved sign for wood work or a sign hanging around the neck of a humorous sculpture?   For a more sophisticated look, have your signs professionally made.   For the   one time expense, a good sign will last you many years.   Repeat your logo or name on printed information about yourself. Have this information   available so that people can take it with them or at least read it easily while standing in your booth.   Always try to have something that has   your contact information on it or your website address. Business cards work great here and can be as simple as home made cards with a touch of your artwork on them, printed on the computer, or ordered inexpensively from companies like Vistaprint.com.   Lots of sales get made,

especially custom orders, after the show.   I've even seen price stickers or stickers on the base or back of a piece that had
 contact info on them. Purchases were taken home or given as gifts which resulted in re-orders for friends and neighbors long after the show was over.

For sales, don't forget that you'll need to make change so visit your bank a couple of days in advance for various denominations of bills and coins.   To keep up with money, the best idea I have ever seen is to have an apron of some sort with several pockets.   Mine is covered with paint so I look the part of a "working artist".   I keep business cards in one pocket, a receipt book and pens in the other, and my change in the third or fourth pocket.   I   don't like to leave a cash box around and I find it easy, especially with several pockets, to make change for a $100 bill by reaching in the left pocket for a $20 bill and in the right pocket for $5 or $1 bills.   No one sees exactly how much money is on my person at any one time and I am able to make quick change.   I can go all the way down to coins if necessary and many times you will need to do this if you have to charge tax or price   your items with odd amounts like $6.50 or $7.25. (More on pricing in chapter 8).   If you have help, you can station someone at a cash box which leaves you free to talk to the customers and make the sales.   In this case, feel free to put them in a lower lawn-type chair at the back of the booth or the front corner where people can easily line up to make their purchases on their way out.   If you have access to use of credit card machines you'll need appropriate electricity or phone connections.   As I write, credit and debit cards get easier and easier to use and you WILL make more sales if you can take them. (Important tip/trick - Check your local banks first for credit card machine rates and availability before you get coerced into a high rate on a credit card machine from an independent company). Unless you just use your phone for credit purchases you'll need a more private space with a flat surface convenient for customers to sign their receipts.

For overnight shows, make sure you have some sort of covering. Most venues have security for overnight events and I've never had anyone steal anything but I always covered everything even if it was just covered with old sheets overnight AND to make things a little harder for the "honest" crooks or early customers that wanted to take a peak before I got there, I clamped the sheets to the table or grid or tent with large spring clamps from the hardware store. These were easily removed as I set up for the day and were an obstacle to potential thieves when I wasn't there.

Now that you have set up your display at home, (RAD) you will need to   figure out how all of this will pack up. Sculptures will need proper packing like newspapers, bubble wrap, or Styrofoam, with strong tape and/or containers that can be repacked for a customer to safely take home or for you to use to   safely return these pieces to your home after the show. Paintings stack up easily when you use bubble wrap, moving blankets, soft towels or those foam "noodles" that are used to insulate pipes or for kids to use in the pool (just slit one side and fit it over the edges of your canvas). Individual products usually fit well in clear plastic containers. You can see what you have at a glance. I've seen more than one artist frantically searching through opaque bins or cardboard boxes to find more products. Your office items can also go in clear boxes. Since you have already set up, just like visualizing the spaces you needed for your art supplies in your studio, you can actually visualize the space you will need for your craft/art set up items. There's nothing worse that just getting a bunch of containers only to find you didn't need half of them or you need to go back to get more. With the set up in place, you can also see how big a trailer you will need or how things will stack up and in which order you will be required to load and unload. Often a twowheeler or foldable luggage carrier could help to transport items into the show. Many outdoor craft fairs will let you drive in, dump your stuff and drive out but only during certain times. After that, you may have to park and transport everything to your space. Make a "plan of attack" and adjust it as you pack and unpack at each show. Before long, things will run smoother and smoother. But no matter how much help you think you might have, plan as closely as you can to making it a one man job. Then, any help you receive will just make it that much easier.

To make sure you don't forget anything, try this little trick I use when I pack for vacations. I take pen and paper and visualize the trip step by step. As I visualize getting into the car I list my purse, sunglasses, credit cards, and money for the trip. I visualize the outfit I will wear and the snacks I'll need as I drive off, listing these items as they come to mind. Next I visualize actually making the first turn in the road where I'll need to list my map and "googled" directions. As I visualize the first night approaching I list my overnight bag with pj's, makeup, comb and brush. For the next morning I visualize needing my toothbrush and toothpaste. Get the picture? As you think through the show, visualize and list everything. Imagine all the steps it will take to set up and make sure you have things like cords to tie down the tent, scissors to cut the cords, tent stakes to tie the cords to, or sandbags to hold the corners down. (See how detailed you need to visualize?) Imagine talking to a customer and needing to write a note on the back of your business card. You'll need pens. What if the customer wants to give you their name and address for future show information? Do you have a sign in book or a notepad to take down this info? Once the sale is made do you have any sacks or containers for the purchase? You can use something as simple as old plastic bags from your local grocer or decorator bags that you can customize yourself or through companies like Store Supply. What if something gets nicked or broken in transit? Do you have a handy repair box with tape and glue and touch up paint? For everything you'll be needing, try to visualize step by step what it will take to have a successful show and then provide for that need. I can't say you'll get it all right the first time but you'll get the knack of it.

Once you've set up at your show, you'll need to start selling. Now, I've seen artists who make a little cubbyhole in the back and practically hide from the customers. Maybe they are customer "shy". Check out your personality and see if this is you. If so, maybe craft/art shows are not the way you want or need to try to sell your artwork. You are your only salesperson so being shy with your customers will definitely hamper your sales. Remember how we talked about being able to say, "I am an artist"? Well, people have a fascinating image of a person who is an artist. Live up to that mystique. Don't just throw on any old outfit for the day. Try wearing an artist's apron, or a beret, or a really flashy outfit. Maybe you can wear one of your creations or something artistic that was created by a fellow artist. You know the "look". Create it and once you have the "look", maybe more of the confidence will come.

Now you are ready to interact with the customer. You've already found a "voice" to your art by finding your style and creating your body of work. Even if you don't feel like you are a great conversationalist, you will find that talking about your artwork is different than trying to make conversation at a party. Ultimately you do not need to do near as much talking as the customer. Your goal, as you engage the customer, is to just listen and respond bringing the conversation back to your artwork at any chance you get. Ask questions that have longer answers than just "yes" or "no". We call this QUALIFYING your customer and learning how to do this will short cut yourself right into a sale. Let me digress a little and lead you through the trick of "QUALIFYING".

First of all QUALIFING can work for every stage of your art career and in every type of sales location. To QUALIFY, never, never, never, assume anything about a customer. You may have heard that clothing makes the man but I can tell you of numerous occasions where I've nearly sold out to the country looking fellow in the overalls (who just happened to own half the county where the fair took place). Never disqualify anyone before you actually qualify him or her. And how do you qualify them? Again, simply engage them in a conversation. Use open ended questions such as "Where are you from?" "How did you hear about the show?" Never, but never, ask "Can I help you?" or ask a question with a "yes" or "no" answer. Even a question like "How are you" that requires a one word answer is a no-no. Make sure the answer to the question has to make the person stop and think a minute and that it's something that you can build on. Make sure they know that you really care about their answer and aren't just swooping in for the sale. Once you try a few questions out for size you'll see what fits. Possible ideas are to think about where the show is located ("Where are ya'll from?"- which could lead to a conversation about their hometown), what the weather is like ("What have you heard about that rainstorm coming our way?" – which could lead to a mutual feeling about the weather) or something relating to your art without seeming pushy ("How did you like that demonstration of the wax resist technique I did? Oh, you didn't get to see it? Well, let me show you a sample of the technique."). Get the idea?

Once you have asked a well phrased question, LISTEN to the customer's answer, build on that answer and respond with your artwork in mind. Always try to bring the conversation back to your artwork. ("So you drove in from Timbuctoo?   I just finished some sketches of that area for my next painting.   It's going to be fashioned after this piece right here.")   Now there's nothing wrong in just having a conversation for the sake of conversation and there's always an opportunity to get to know a new friend at your shows or to share "war stories" with your art booth neighbor, but you are here at this show on this day to make some sales. Sure, you had a great time talking all day but were you and your new friend so caught up in your conversation that three other customers have come and gone with out so much as a "howdy do"?

A real tip to QUALIFYING is to listen for clues about the customer like where they are from, what kind of family they have, what kind of job, hobby, or retirement goals they are pursuing.   Respond with a slant toward your artwork.   For example, "Yes that's a lovely place, I was there once painting 'such and such'" or "Yes, I'd love to have an opportunity to visit there to get ideas for my newest sculptures. Can you tell me some of the prettiest landmarks there?" or "Yes, I'm retired from a similar business. I took up my artwork during the final years that I was there and I haven't looked back" or "You know, my kids are always the ones that inspire me too. I did this metal sculpture after seeing my kids do just what your kids did."   Get the idea again?   Just listen and listen with an ear toward your work and the next thing you know, as Jack White said in his book, The Magic of Selling Art, you have helped them find just what they were looking for.   And in the conversation you've taken a huge step toward your sale by

74

beginning to get a feel for their disposable income. Knowing a little about their income will help you relate this particular sale to the possible choices of the $1 items or the $1000 items. For example, did they just return from a vacation in Europe or a vacation where they stayed home and did some badly needed home repairs? Knowing this information saves you from trying to under or over sell and/or from wasting anyone's time.

And qualifying is not over there. You can lead the horse to water but you can't make him drink unless you know how to ask for the sale and close the sale. "Oh, wait", you say, "I'm not a salesman, (said as if the word salesman were a bad word), I'll just let the customer decide on their own". Well, you know, sometimes they do decide on their own but in all my years of art sales especially in a gallery-type situation I've found that 90% of the time people are unsure of their decision making process when it comes to selecting art. The statement "Let me bring my wife back to see what she thinks" is a dead sale every time. It's near impossible to get two people to decide on something that is purchased, not as a need, but as a desire or "want" like art. But they need the reinforcement that the decision that they are making is a good one. So, LISTEN and you'll hear a positive statement about the work. Agree with their statement; confirm that they have made a good/excellent choice. Talk about how this piece is the right piece. Help them imagine it in their home. Ask specifics like "which room do you think you'll hang this piece?" or "Do you think the greens in this piece or that piece would match your office décor better?" OR if you have yourself set up appropriately, you may ask "Would you like to charge this or would you like to use our payment plan?" or "Would you like for me to ship this piece or hold it for you until the end of the show?" (By the way, NEVER hold something for someone while they think about purchasing it., only hold it if it's been paid for). If you're not set up this way how about saying, "Would you like to pay cash or would a check work better for you?" And then make sure that you have the correct information on a check. (Side note here: Yes I've had bad checks come to me through a crafts or art show but I had all their information from their driver's license plus business and home phone numbers. With contact information all I usually had to do was to make one call after receiving a "bad check" and it would be straightened out. I mean, not many people write a bad check on purpose for art . . . food, maybe. . . but seldom a work of art). If you are really uncomfortable taking anything but cash put up a big sign that says "Cash Only" but I can guarantee that the more payment methods you take, the more sales you will make. You must weigh the chances for the venue (church bazaar versus street beer and music festival) and the cost of the item.

Once you start to feel comfortable making the sale, try for an "up sale". For smaller items, did you mention how attractive a pair would look or do you have a special two for one offer that would allow them to purchase more for gifts. Perhaps you can offer a free frame or pack of note cards with any purchase over X amount. Watch what the big department stores do and though you may feel like you're selling used cars,

76

remember that everyone loves a bargain or a "deal".

Now that's QUALIFYING and knowing and mastering it's techniques will not only gain you sales, but make you more comfortable in your sales position. After all, you are an artist first and by need or desire you are a salesman second. Remember your chapter 1 statement "I am an artist working as a salesman" not a salesman who is "pushing" your art.

Back to our show, (sounds like we just had a "qualifying commercial") once you've sold your goods and the show is over you may be asked to submit taxes to the show coordinators. If you have set yourself up with your own tax ID number you'll pay your own taxes later. Sometimes you must state this on a form for their purposes. Sometimes there is a percent owed to the venue (most often a percent that goes to the church or charity that supported the show). Finalize all paperwork so that you have cooperated fully. Make sure the venue has your contact info for future shows (whether or not you think you will come back) because sometimes they share your info with better shows. And finally, be sure to keep copies of all transactions.

The trick to a successful art/craft show is going to be in the planning and organizing. If this is not your best "fit", either work at it or select another way to showcase your art such as . . .

CONTESTS OR JURIED SHOWS

Contests can be places to sell but are most often just contests with prizes. To enter you must fill out the proper forms and submit those forms in a timely manner. Read the forms carefully. If they require slides, you must submit slides, if a CD, then you must submit a CD. Submitting to contests is a good training ground for submissions to shows and galleries. Once you get the contest submissions done and done correctly, then you can easily submit to almost anything.

Now, a word about contests before I give you the "how to's". I personally, am not a contest fan. I have achieved a confidence in my work whereby I really need no confirmation from a "judge" as to whether or not my work is contest worthy. I sell to the public and they are the ones to whom I target my work and I have yet had any customer ask for my list of contest winnings. And this book is about selling, not about awards and honors though they may come in handy on your resume.

I am reminded of the ceramic doll a friend created that won Best of Show in a local art fair. It was prominently displayed with its' award winning ribbon in her craft booth with a comparable price to her other pieces. Even though she sold many other pieces over the years at her shows, she still has the award winner. Though the doll was skillfully made, it never connected with the customer, blue ribbon or no blue ribbon. Awards don't necessarily tip the tower toward the sale. Besides, judges for contests are only one person or one

78

group of people with their own opinion(s) and unless I have researched the judge(s), have great respect for them, or just really feel like I need the validation, I don't enter.   Juried shows are much the same.   Again, someone approves or disapproves of your work and therefore validates it by putting it in a particular show or awarding the piece some sort of recognition.   The recognition becomes the   "sale" in most cases.   Again, this is great for your resume but doesn't mean much to the customer. Most of the time the customer has no idea or even cares that it was an honor just to get juried into the show.   They may come to that particular show because of the high caliber of artwork but that doesn't mean they will buy more artwork. And if sales is your goal, you can waste a lot of time entering, worrying about getting rejected and/or shipping work to their shows upon acceptance, following their rules, etc etc etc.

That said, on the other side of the coin, I have one artist friend who enters each and every contest and juried show that he can afford.   His theory is that if he is accepted into a contest in some well established art community, that he has a greater chance of being "discovered".   He is of the mindset that having that one selected/juried piece in a   show   in a market like Chicago or New York will "make" him.   So far, he's just mostly out a lot of entry fees, travel expenses and/or shipping costs for the pieces to go both ways, to and from the show. Perhaps the best thing that may come from contests and juried shows is that they can be   a great way to get the validation that you need in order   to call yourself an artist.

But they are just as easily a way to devaluate yourself as an artist if you don't win or get juried in. So prepare yourself either way as you submit.

Still interested in contests and juried shows? Magazines abound with contests. You'll find the best contests through art magazines or magazines that specialize in your craft. You can also find them through local shops and national chains. To become abreast of the latest contests and juried shows it helps to become a member of a craft or art organization either locally, statewide, or nationally or even internationally. Even if you aren't a "joiner" having your name on their membership lists will get you first hand info on contests and juried shows. Becoming an active member gets you not only the first hand info but the real "insider" info. From other's experiences you find out which ones are worth entering, who the judges are, what they are looking for, and even which ones may be "rigged" (take this with a grain of salt for you may be talking to the one person who got juried out of the show or lost the contest). Individuals in these groups also know the best photographers for your work if you need one (often one of the members themselves will give you a huge discount) and the where, when, and how of the event. If the event has entry deadlines, sometimes several people in a group or club go together to deliver each other's application or artwork. I've had to take my work to the judges at 9 am on a Sat. and then retrieve it later that day when the jury had made their decisions. In a case like this often I would pick up or drop off

80

another artist's   work along with mine and they would return the favor by picking mine up with theirs in the afternoon.

If you do get juried out try to see the show or order a catalogue of the show.   That way you can see   what got juried in.   It's up to you if this means enough to cause you to change or   defend your own work.   And remember that if you get juried out you have to realize that   you might have been on the cutting edge of getting in but you'll never know it.   Perhaps you may have just not appealed to the judges' love of abstracts with your photo-realism or you might have just slipped up on having your frame ½ inch too big.   I once judged a contest where the 1st prize winner had to be eliminated because they had not attended the required number of association meetings. That artist will never know why they didn't even place in that contest.

Sometimes just losing a contest or being juried out can be the best education because you'll get a judgment call from an unbiased person or art group but don't expect an explanation.   Judges seldom have the time to evaluate the pieces of the show.   You'll just need to look at the winning pieces yourself and make what conclusions you can.

ORGANIZATIONS

I mentioned ORGANIZATIONS as a way to learn about and be more successful in CONTESTS and JURIED SHOWS but they can also be successful means of selling your art.

First, because of the networking you can do through an ORGANIZATION. Becoming a member of an organization gives you insider information on everything from shops to shows to galleries to just the art market in general. You'll learn from member's experiences, workshops that they sponsor, speakers they attract, and just being on their mailing lists exposes you to all sorts of venues for showing your work especially at the local level. Plus creating a relationship with other artists gives you opportunities to split booth rents, learn from other's experiences, find out the good and bad shows or galleries, what art events are coming up and create even more opportunities for networking with people in the business of art.

Look for local groups in your yellow pages or local papers. Community centers are often the meeting places and/or have contact info for groups. National groups can be found in major publications of your art or craft. Most have websites. Go online to find out which ones you might like to join. Be aware that sometimes they have high membership fees (the higher they are the more they offer the members) and/or have a jury selection process to be a member (more bragging rights). Mostly ORGANIZATIONS will open the door to opportunities. Working these opportunities through the skills learned in this book will determine how far you can go with this information.

RETAIL

Another artist friend of mine loads up his truck with all

of the paintings that will fit. As he drives around town and notices a store that might be interested in selling his work he stops and goes in, starts a conversation with the owner if possible, and drops off a few pieces for sale. I accuse him of needing a bumper sticker that says "I brake for art sales". It's not something I feel comfortable doing but it works tremendously well for him. Again, there are pros and cons to this and you have to find out what works for you. Early on, he just took pictures of his work with him and this worked almost as well as loading his car. But you see, what makes this work so well for him is that he is a natural born salesman. I went with him one day to see how all this worked for him. Here's how the day went:

Loaded with pieces of his work, he stopped in a gift/interior decoration showroom. It was a weekday so the place wasn't crowded and he walked through the shop much like a customer would at first. Once he determined that yes, this shop has original artwork and that his artwork would "fit" he approached the counter and struck up a conversation about the artwork in particular. Clerks, sensing he is a customer are usually very informative about where and how they get their artwork. Sometimes they even know what the shop charges in commission. If so, he has all the information he needs and can proceed to inquire about who he needs to talk to in order to show some of his own work for possible consideration. At that point he either gets a chance to speak to the manager or at least make an appointment to see the manager. He never leaves without one or the other (see I told you he was a go-getter type).

Let me digress just a moment and elaborate on the part about his art "fitting" the shop. This is such an important aspect of any location that sells your artwork. The obvious tip here it to go see the location even if you are "seeing" it online. Whether it's a gallery or decorator store, you can tell that if all they show is abstract art, then you will be wasting your time if all you have is extreme realism. Likewise if all they show in the gallery is southwestern art, your sculpted lighthouses aren't going to help them or you make sales. Use logic and highly evaluate how your work would fit in before you waste anyone's time. I used to have artists call up my gallery all the time wanting to bring in artwork. My first question was, "Have you seen our gallery?" If not, the first thing I would tell them to do would be to go online to see work by the other artists that we represented and/or to visit the gallery. Even if you are from out of town, there's a way to check out the gallery or shop. Think of it this way, wouldn't you be embarrassed to have your Michelangelo quality work sitting in the middle of empty coke cans decorated with pom poms? Or equally embarrassed that your highly popular pom pom coke cans are shuffled to the back room on a bottom shelf in a high end art gallery? So make sure you are not wasting anyone's time, especially your own, making an appointment, dragging your work in, talking to the owner, just to look ridiculous and be rejected all at the same time. I mean if your work is what they are looking for 10 times out of 10 a retail establishment will

84

take your work.   It doesn't cost them anything since they will probably be working with you on a commission basis.   You just have to give them something they can sell.

Once your work "fits" a retail shop and is accepted, this can be a really effective selling location.   A mandatory tip here is to   make sure you have some sort of inventory of the pieces you give them so that they don't get "lost" in the shuffle.   Retail establishments rotate all of their merchandise so much that even the manager or owner may not be able to locate your pieces as little as   a week later without some hunting.   Who's got a bigger stake in keeping up with it?   You do.   AND honest or not, places "lose" pieces by loaning them out on consignment, shuffling new merchandise around, etc. With computers and digital cameras today, there is no excuse for not knowing where your artwork is even if it's spread out through several shops, stores, and venues.

A good method of inventory is to take a picture of each piece as you create it.   (RAD) Have it printed and/or download it to your computer as soon as it's created.   Put all pertinent information   on the picture or picture page (size, title, medium,   completion date, etc).   You can also include any specific notes you would like to make about the piece (theme of the   series, models name, etc).   An abstract artist friend of mine finds this helpful for another reason – he titles his work Red Abstract #1, Red Abstract #2, etc.   When he creates a new piece he has to try to remember, somehow, what number he is on.   His digital images let him know the next number in the series.   For multiples like having created 15 corn husk dolls, you can take a picture of one or the entire grouping making note of the specific number of pieces in this set/series/or run.   For example: 15 corn husk dolls, 3 with blue skirts, 10 with yellow skirts and 2 with orange skirts.

Even with computers, I still like to print out a "hard copy" photo of my pieces.   I do this so that when I have pieces accepted into retail/gallery/shows, I can physically pull that picture and insert it into a file/envelope/clear folder marked for that location.   If it sells, I take it out and put it in my "sold" file along with information about the selling price and information about the buyer if possible.   If I take it from one location to another I physically switch it from one envelope/file to another.   I could also keep all this information on my lap top and take it with me to the shops but I like having a "hard copy", too.

For example: I walk into a shop and they take four specific paintings of mine for resale.   I have pictures of each piece with specifics including the price I expect to get for the piece in a notebook with clear plastic sleeves.   I pull the pictures of each piece they take   and   have the owner fill out my "agreement form" (a sample agreement form can be found in the appendix).   Then I put the "agreement form" with the pictures in one separate envelope or sleeve.   If I send a painting to a group show, I make note of the entry form or location and put that picture in a separate sleeve.   I keep all of this in one book so that I can go home and arrange all of this in my computer.   But even if I didn't put it in the computer, I have all my paintings photographed and I know where each

86

one is located.

From experiences in my own   art gallery I learned that many artists don't bother doing this.   At one time I was cleaning out the back room and found literally a dozen or more works of art that were left from group shows or from artists that moved out of state.   Sometimes I could contact the artist to retrieve their work but sometimes their contact information was lost.   I never intended to "own" these pieces but no one ever inquired after years of them being stored in the gallery's back room.

With my files in hand and a date on my calendar to remind me to check back regularly or to contact them at the end of an arrangement, I can easily pull my photos out, identify everything that did not sell, and hold the owner/manager accountable for these sales and for anything that is "lost".   If there's a problem,   there's little arguing with these photos and good records including signatures.   I also keep track of how much commission I should be getting, amounts that the artwork sold for in these venues, contact people, customer inquiries, and customers to whom they sold your artwork.   Don't be surprised if many times the gallery or shop will not share customer's names with you.   It's usually a standard business policy not to.   This is to prevent customers and artists from contacting each other directly, trying to leave the shop out of the transaction.   Yes, this would save the customer the gallery commission, and   it might not   make any difference to the amount you take home from the sale but it's ethically wrong.

If you contact a customer, arrange a sale and leave the gallery out, believe me, the gallery or shop will find out and not only will be you "out" of that venue but word travels. You could find yourself without representation anywhere.

What your shop or gallery is doing for you for the commission that they may charge is advertising, bringing in the customers, acting as salesmen for your work, providing a building with utilities, bring in the buying public and much, much, more. If the gallery or shop is doing their job, you are "free" to create so the commission is well worth it.

If, on the other hand, you feel the shop or venue is not bringing in the customers, or they are keeping your work in the backroom seldom showing it out front, and/or disrespecting your work in any way, then you either re-negotiate their commission or your arrangement with them or pull out of the venue completely. Even if this is the case, you never go behind their back to make a sale. If they know and have confidence that you are working with them cooperatively, then they should be doing all that is in their power to promote and sell your work. If not, selling behind their backs is just two wrongs which don't make a "right".

Commissions with retail establishments will vary from 10 – 60%. My rule of thumb for establishing sales price is by establishing my bottom line price which I divide by the percent that I would get. You'll find a detailed formula for this in Chapter 8.

Sometimes a venue just wants to pay you outright for the piece and you will get your bottom line price (or better if you negotiate) and that's it. Over and done. Most of the time, however, you will essentially "give" them your work for the commission upon sale. Their good word, your inventory control, and the paperwork you sign is all the agreement you have. (See how important paperwork can be?) Sometimes they will and sometimes they won't have insurance to cover loss, fire, or damage. Most "lower end" shops will not have any insurance to cover this loss. It's up to you as to what chance you want to take with that knowledge. It always depends on how badly you need the money. If there's a chance to sell that piece in their place for a really nice price, and the place and paperwork look as good and as safe as you can imagine, then you may choose to leave the piece even without insurance. If there's an act of God and/or a true accident you may have to chalk it up to "well, it was just two hours of fun and $12 worth of canvas". If your work means more than that to you maybe this is not the venue for your art or perhaps you're lucky enough to be able to get an affordable policy from your home owner's insurance. Until you become a "famous" artist you may only get replacement value from an insurance company such as the cost of the canvas and paint or the photographic paper and frame but that's better than nothing. Once you begin selling regularly and have records to prove the value of your work, you may join the Picasso's and Warhol's of the world with hundreds of dollars in true replacement value. So start keeping that paperwork. (RAD)

Another thing to remember in retail is that your art is not the focal point as much as the whole setting around your art. Your painting might be hung above a decorator table with a big vase of flowers in front or your sculpture may be on a dining room table complete with place mats and dishes. A decorator will be showcasing the whole look along with your piece. Your piece may also be transported several times outside the shop to individual's homes for two to three days for their final approval. In some high end stores you can restrict your pieces to limited time out for approval or refuse to allow it out but the harder you are to get along with the harder the sale is to make for you and for them.

An important thing to think about once you have settled into selling in a retail shop is that once you've sold there, you may never get to sell "higher". By that I mean, you may never get a gallery or museum to take your work seriously. Who wants to create a whole show around artwork that was sold at Martha's Gift Emporium just last year?

Likewise, if you are stopping at every little gift and decorator showroom, one question you may be asked is "where else are you selling your work?" If you just dropped off two pieces three blocks over, then this retailer isn't going to want to sell your work. They want the most unique and exclusive work that they can get. If one or more stores already carry your work you are no longer unique and their prices have to vary (usually making them less) in order to make the sale. Your best bet, when shopping around for a retail establishment to showcase your work is to visit all the stores that you think would be able to sell for you. Make a list of the shops you like from the best or highest end shop to the less expensive gift-type shops.   Then try to arrange sales with the "best" shop first. If they say no, go to the next best and so on until you find a shop that would like to represent you.

Another trick for finding a good   retail establishment can be found every time you go on vacation. Check out the retail establishments   while there and you may find that if you keep track of your expenses a large part of the cost of your vacation can be deducted as a business expense especially once you have established one of those shops as a sales place for your work.   You may have to return regularly to this great vacation location   in order to replenish the artwork that they have sold, but you wanted to go back anyway, didn't you? Now you have a wonderful excuse to visit again and a wonderful place to sell especially if you feel inclined to paint or sculpt or photograph some of the local tourist attractions. Don't forget, as in any city or location, to take a little time to visit all the possible shops first, rank them in order of your most desired location to the least desired location, and then visit the most important shop first.   At least this way you didn't mess up by going   to Joe's Junktiques first where he bought your work outright for $50 per item before you visited La Galleria and missed a chance to sell for 50% commission of $500.

COFFEE SHOPS, LOBBIES, ETC.

When you are just starting out in the art field, there

aren't many doors that are as wide open to an unknown artist as coffee shops, local libraries, community centers, public lobbies, restaurants, and waiting rooms. These are great places to "test the waters" with a show of your artwork. It helps you not only practice the art of display but also helps you get your initial public reaction to the work. To get started simply drop by any of these venues and speak to a manager or representative. They either have a regular application process that is truly easy (show your work and book a date) or they may even sign you up for a show without even seeing your work. Coffee shops in particular like to decorate for free (with your artwork) and libraries like to give the locals a chance to use their community rooms. They may even allow you to have an opening reception of sorts and/or they may do a reception and some advertising for you. These places are usually pretty easy going about the hanging of the work (they'll give you a list of rules if they aren't) and you get the experience of creating and exhibiting your own show. It's not a great bragging right to say you are currently showing at Charlie's Buffet on Hwy 12 but it gives you a chance to create a show, see what it takes to have enough cohesive work to present to the public, advertise your "show", get the public's response, and maybe, just maybe, get "discovered" by that big town art gallery owner who just happened to stop by for a cup of coffee.

GALLERIES

This brings us to the highest or next to highest venue on our list of places to show. ART GALLERIES. I would consider owning your own art gallery(s) as being the highest but let's not get ahead of ourselves. Remember, also, that being in or owning a gallery may not even be a goal that you want to achieve. If the gallery route is the one you want to achieve, though, here are some excellent tips and tricks to getting there.

First, and most importantly, we are assuming that you have a body of work that you are proud of. Secondly, this body of work has something that connects it whether it be style or theme, or color. And third, there's a theme or aspect of the work that just screams promotional and show ideas. All of this is already accomplished by creating that body of work and seriously assessing it. (RAD)

Once you have done that, we are assuming that you've visited either in person or online, the galleries in which you want to have a show. (RAD) Just as you learned about the retail establishments, you'll need to rank these galleries from your favorite and possibly the most famous gallery to the lesser known or newer galleries. (RAD) Perhaps in your visits you've already created a relationship with the owner/manager even if it's just coming to their openings and/or shows and making light conversation (remember the importance of networking). Maybe you've even had a chance to mention that you are an artist and how much you enjoy their gallery for whatever reason.   You might mention that you feel a connection with this particular gallery but whatever you do, never push your artwork on them.   Matter of fact, even when I mention that I'm an artist and I get a conversation going with the gallery rep, I've never come out and asked them for a show. I may tell them that I'm working on a series right now, or having the pieces photographed or adding to a body of work so that the gallery rep follows up the conversation with a comment about how they would like to see that work, but unless they ask I seldom push it.   You see, as a gallery owner, having someone ask for a show used to "put me on the spot". I solved that problem by whipping out an application for a show that I created and required them to submit a proposal. First, it helped me see how serious they really were, kept me from saying "no" to beginner artists or friends who wanted a show, and gave me time to pick and choose the best shows. Remember the gallery owner is not in the specific business of promoting art but of selling art and though one should lead to the other, they are not the same.   Also, in my conversations as an artist with gallery owners I find that often they like to think that they are "discovering" you.   As you converse with the gallery owners and reps that you meet, you may feel more comfortable   asking them if they would like to see your work but I'm more about the psychology of having them ask me to see it.   It's your call.

What if you haven't found a gallery, don't have any nearby, or want to start marketing your art out of your area? That means you can't establish the person to person

94

relationship anyway, so your initial contacts and "conversations" will probably be online or by mail with a few phone calls thrown in once the submission process has begun.

To find galleries, the best resource guide is the most current issue of <u>Artists' Market</u>. This book comes out each year. You will need the most current year even if you have to order it because galleries come and go quickly especially in this economy. This is a huge book but will be worth the time to read through from cover to cover highlighting specific things you find useful. (RAD) The book not only lists galleries, the work they show and how to submit your work but it also has personal stories of artists who have done something successful to create or market their artwork. You'll get tons of ideas from this. The book is divided into several other sections besides just GALLERIES. Some of these sections will open doors for you in the marketing of your art through prints, greeting card illustrations, posters, and other shops and shows. No matter what section interests you there will be info about the gallery or venue, contact information and most importantly a list of the kind of artwork they want to show and sell along with detailed instructions for submission requirements. The book is huge but like I said, it is well worth the time to make lists or highlight any and all venues that you think might like your work. Then, just like visiting the galleries in town, go online to actually see the gallery or businesses that you've chosen. Look for quality in the location, how old the business is, and most importantly, what type of artwork they represent. Hopefully you've already eliminated the galleries that specialize in abstract art if you only do extreme realism and the southwestern galleries because you only do oriental themed artwork. Make your list of venues from favorite to least favorite depending on location (remember you have to get the artwork to them), commission rate, look of the gallery, or whatever is most important to you in a gallery or company, then submit.

Most of the submission requirements are very similar. I've found that though the first submission may take time and effort, in these days of computers, once you have the first one done, the rest will be simply a matter of changing a few words or pictures and printing and sending the application on. The following list is required for most gallery submissions either online or in person.

QUERY LETTER
RESUME
ARTIST'S STATEMENT
BROCHURES
PHOTOS
REVIEWS

Then, if you are chosen for an interview, you may need a PORTFOLIO of slides or photos with size and price to show them in person. Detailed explanations of each item follow and you will find examples of a query letter, resume, and artist's statement in the appendix.

Your QUERY LETTER should be just like a query

letter for a job interview. You can find a form on your computer that will do just fine. Don't try to get all artsy with the font. Stay as business-like as you can. The computer forms and your query letter will possibly have a heading of sorts and a date and may or may not have the address and contact person's name. If you know the contact person, by all means use it. If not, a simple "To Whom it May Concern" will suffice. In the body of the letter, state who you are, what you do, and why you've picked their venue. The more you know about their desires (from the Artists' Market book plus personal and online visits) the more you can explain to them how your work may fit their requirements. Don't get too creative with this letter. The venues you will be approaching are business oriented. The owner/manager may love art but he's probably more left brained in a right brained art world.

RESUMES and BIOS are two totally different animals. To create a resume think of a job resume. Again, you can find a template on your computer. On the resume you will list your contact info, educational background (even if it doesn't apply to art), work skills (that may or may not apply to art), and then your art activities. The art activities can be such things as shows, awards, other representing galleries, owners of collections of your pieces, etc. You can head each of these sections just as you did educational background or work skills. If you won or were juried into a contest, this is where you need to brag. If you had a one man show (even if it was at the coffee house) this is where you need to list it.

Remember that   the gallery rep has to be able to "sell" you to the public.   This is what I mean when I said that the third item you need to get a gallery show is to have something about your work that just screams show promotion or advertising.   That special something may be found in your resume. For example, knowing that you were the photographer for Fed Ex for 30 years, photographing planes and spending your spare time photographing exotic locations or knowing that you graduated from Yale with a doctorate and have switched your job skills to art are items that peak the interest of not only the gallery   representative but also the public in general. ("Where did you get to go to take pictures? Oh, so that's why we have this wonderful show of lions, tigers, and bears in Africa."   "Why did you chuck it all and become an artist?" Thousands of people wish they could chuck their job and become an artist.   Ho did you do it and why?) And I know this sounds callous, but to the gallery representative,   knowing that you are a retired lawyer, doctor or famous entertainer could mean that you have   friends who may be inclined to have enough money and know you well enough to buy your work making for an automatic customer base. The gallery or art company you are working with is supposed to have their own client list but expanding their list through your contacts helps everyone.   Sometimes, in the business of gallery ownership, when there was a toss up of which artist should show in which months, the artist's background (for ease in creating a publicity "angle") and/or the idea that they had their own client base tipped the margin into their favor.   Many

98

times some of a gallery's   best clients won't even come see your show but will take the word of the gallery about your work so give them something to talk about.   It's a crazy business, so for the resume and for all requests that may sound strange coming from the gallery, you just need to remember to think in terms of business and what will "catch on" about your work and include that information whenever possible.

The BIO is a biography of your life in an abbreviated form.   Here's another place to find something special about you or your work.   Even if you feel that   your life hasn't been much worth talking about, (school, then college, work, then family, etc) then think again.   Are you full blooded Cherokee, or of Italian descent?   You can start your bio with this.   It adds interest to you, your art, and why you are an artist at this stage of your life.   I've even found successful artists who used something as humble as the background of being especially poor or "just" a housewife, or   "just" a salesman to their advantage.   Think of what you did as a poor child that influenced your art, or what you found out about yourself as a housewife that influenced your art, or the places you've traveled as a salesman that influenced your art.   Always relate back to how your life influenced your art BUT keep from making this an artists' statement.   Try to answer these types of questions in your bio:

Where was I was born?

What is my heritage or background?

Where did I go to school?

Where did I learn my art skills?

Where have I traveled?

How did I get to be an artist?

You may be able to think of more questions to ask yourself. And your answers may surprise you or lead you into other interesting aspects of your life in art. Even a simple answer like being a self taught artist can be depicted in a positive light. Keep the bio brief but interesting. Set your goal at no more than 1 full page for the bio.

The ARTIST'S STATEMENT is you talking about your work. Imagine being interviewed at your opening reception. The reporter asks you "Why do you create" or "What is unique about your work or this show". In a sentence or a paragraph or two, explain yourself. Again, be brief but interesting.

BROCHURES and BUSINESS CARDS are usually optional but not beyond your doing with minimal computer skills. Anyone can print out business cards on the computer and companies like Vistaprint.com will supply you with free or nearly free business cards, brochures, postcards, and more that are easily created using templates online. With companies like Vistaprint you can even create promotional items like pens, bags, bumper stickers, etc. These are perfect for craft and art shows and for leaving with gift shops. For gallery or fine art business use, try not to get too "cute-sy" with the ideas.   Keep yourself as business-like as possible unless your art just screams commercialism.   For example,   if you are selling "Cuddly Critters" at craft shows, get yourself a couple of "Cuddly Critters" t-shirts to wear at the show or hand out "Cuddly Critters" pens and notepads as freebies with purchase.   But t-shirts and hats won't be of much use in an upscale gallery.   Expensive printing costs are a thing of the past and do it yourself jobs on the computer are surprisingly professional looking so there's really no excuse for not having some sort of promotional material for you, your art, your shows, etc.

PHOTOS of your work for art business submissions are usually in digital forms these days.   As of about 5 years ago some galleries were asking for slides or accepting slides of your work.   Hardly any gallery even has a slide projector any more.   But everyone has computers.   If you don't know how to photograph your work or create a CD you can pay for this service,   take classes to learn,   or through a group or organization you may find a free or inexpensive workshop or helper to show you how to do these things.   I've found that an 8 mega-pixel or higher camera, proper lighting, and my home computer has helped me create a presentation to rival any I've seen submitted to me as a gallery owner or juror in art contests. The CD photos must have at least the title, medium, and size for each piece.   And you will also need a contact sheet (check out the programs on your computer) to go along with the CD that has coordinating titles, mediums and size.   The contact sheet is mandatory with the CD. All of these things sound daunting until you explore what you can do or what you can learn to do so don't be intimidated about the process.

After you have submitted all of the above information as required by the venue, you may be called in for an appointment and a personal interview. If so, you may need to take these same pictures and print them out. Always have title, medium and size next to the pictures on the CD's and/or on the photos somehow (again, check out programs on your computer). Many times the art venue will want the prices of the pieces too. You can either add the prices to the program before you print or you can add a separate sheet. A separate sheet will allow you to change or refigure these prices for different venues or for different submissions/requirements (do they want your bottom line price or the retail price? – more about pricing in chapter 8).

All of the above information is either required or optional and yes, it will take a little time to create a proper presentation packet but once it is done, especially if you were able to learn to do it all yourself, it is as easy as click, type corrections, and print to submit to various venues over and over.

As far as cost for all this submission material, you can literally do everything on a shoe string budget. As of the publication date of this book I added up everything including the bubble wrap envelope for mailing the entire packet, and came up with an outlay of less than $200. The breakdown

102

included 250 free business cards and 50 free brochures from Vistaprint, a CD with case, and the paper and ink it took to print out all information on my computer. I not only had one good packet to send out but I still had enough supplies left over for at least five more complete submissions and lots of cards and brochures for other uses or for other applications. All I need to do is change some wording here and there in my computer, print out the paperwork, insert my CD, cards, and brochures, and I've got another packet all ready to submit.

WEBSITES

First of all, let me tell you that you will rarely sell your artwork off your website. If you want to sell you artwork online try e-bay or Etsy (awesome for crafts). Even with these, don't expect to make a fortune but also don't expect to have to pay a whole lot to try.

So why have a website? The best thing about having one is that it's so easy to show someone your work. I've gotten several inquiries for potential shows, seminars, and workshops from the information on my website. And, just a basic computer knowledge will get you started. Currently, there are free websites through places you can google (even through Google, itself) but when I created my site I was directed to one of the easiest I've ever had the privilege of working with and that is Artspan.com. It was designed for the artist and art gallery in mind. In fact I used it for both my personal and gallery business use for two reasons. 1) It was easy to create and 2) It was easy to maintain. I mean you can get your brother in law's nephew's second cousin to create a site for you but how are you going find him to update it? One of the most important aspects of your site is that it stays updated. That's what is so great about Artspan. It uses a template that is so easy to use that I seriously completely designed my website while watching the super bowl game one year. If I need to change it I go online, click a button to delete something, click a button to download, and click a button to completely change anything including the color, font or look of the site. There are a ton of different things you can do to the site once you get really good at working with it like adding animation and music but I recommend not worrying about getting too fancy. Sometimes all that "extra" stuff just makes it harder to download for you and the viewer and all the whistles and bells can overpower your artwork. Remember, the artwork is the main thing you want to show off, not your computer tricks.

Here's an example of how a website can help you. Let' say you met someone at a social gathering or just on the street and the conversation rolls around to "what do you do?" Remember the old hemming and hawing you use to do about your artwork? Well, now, since you have applied RAD to the steps of this book, you are prepared to tell them, "I am an artist, a painter who works in oils. I'm currently working on a series of Italian landscapes." And if, true to form, the listener is interested enough to want to see your work, what do you do in

104

the middle of the subway? If you have a current showing of your work, you can whip out a postcard or direct them to the shop or gallery. If not, you can easily direct them to your website. If you've made your domain name easy to remember (please try) like YourName.com (rather than Yo_ur-middle-name_and-last-Na_me.com) they can go home and immediately get online to find your site. It you make it more complicated, you may have to write it down or better yet, whip out a business card with the website address.

Once they log on to your site, they should find pictures of your current work, photos of the latest series or show you did, contact information for commissions or classes. If you have a good site you can add lots of other categories and even a pay pal system to sell directly from the site.

Some important tips about selling on your site - Be prepared to figure out shipping and handling fees if you do make a sale. And use Pay Pal or figure out a safe way to get payment first. Make sure the customer is legit. (More than one artist has been duped by "customers" sending bogus checks for larger than the amount needed and requesting a refund of the balance along with the artwork). And be aware that selling through your site can be in direct conflict with any gallery or shop trying to sell you work. Even if a gallery hasn't made you "exclusive" they won't appreciate you selling the work that they have on their walls through your website.

I personally make no attempts to list prices or sell on my site. I use the site basically for promotion only. When I have a representing shop, show or gallery, I plug the venue on a page listed "Purchase Information" or "Representation". The venues appreciate the fact that I direct sales to them and my site looks a lot more professional. Check out the sites of some of the more famous artists that you know and you'll see "models" for your website. (RAD)

Chapter 8: Pricing and Presentation

Of all the questions I am asked about marketing or selling your artwork, the most common is "How do I set my price?" There are several different trips and tricks to get the price you want and this also varies by the location in which you are selling. But there are some basics that are universal and create a good starting point in becoming consistent and realistic with your pricing.

First of all, we'll assume that you are an "unknown" artist. Perhaps you've never sold a piece of your art in your life. But you know it's good, either by your standards or the opinion of friends and relatives. Perhaps you've compared your skill level to those who are already selling and you are ready to try it yourself.

Again, assuming that you don't have a reputation yet, you have hopefully figured out the venue in which you will be selling your artwork. (RAD) If it's to be sold directly through you and no other gallery or expenses are involved then one price will suffice. All you have to do is figure out what you want for the piece over an above the expenses of its' creation. We call this our bottom line and this number will be important to any pricing method you choose to use. We are also assuming that you have also prepared yourself for pricing by visiting the venues that you hope will sell your work and taken Into account what price range comparable pieces are getting. (RAD)   No matter how much ego you have involved in your pieces ("mine are way better") your opinion and the opinion of the customer may differ.   And when your work compares favorably with a lower priced item it must be at least two times better to charge twice the price, three times better to charge three times the price, etc.

Keeping that in mind, having used RAD to get your body of work that is ready to sell, there are several formulas, tips and tricks that you can use to start pricing your work. I have divided the ideas into various art mediums.   Read through all the mediums even if you don't think the ideas would apply to your work because the reasoning and tips and tricks for each one may help create a whole new formula of your own creation which would make both you and your customers comfortable.   Having a formula will also help you easily and adequately adjust your prices if necessary for the venue, multiple sales, special deals, increased popularity of your work or the changes in the general economy.

The first step to pricing is to find your "Bottom Line".

There are many ways to find the "Bottom Line"   in your artwork.   I am going to concentrate on two Methods. Work through each of these methods to find which works best for you and/or what ideas you can adapt to your own particular artwork. (RAD)

108

Method A involves three basic steps. The first step is to figure your actual supply costs. This means you'll need to keep receipts for everything from actual supplies to booth rent to gas for transportation. Total all these expenses and then divide by how many items you made.

For example if you have a $40 total for all the supplies it takes to make 20 items, then you can easily figure that it takes $2 worth of supplies for each item. When you have several items which each took various amounts of supplies it gets more complicated but even painters or sculptors can figure out about how much of a tube of paint or how many boxes of nails might be needed for a project.

I have a portrait artist friend who buys new paint brushes for each portrait. That's easy enough to figure his brush supply costs but you may have to actually take the cost of a brush, or a wood chisel, and figure how long this supply will last before you have to buy another one or have this one repaired. As you work and keep receipts (RAD) you will find it easier to figure your supply costs. You may even find that there is an average cost per month for the expense of new supplies and repair costs. You can use this average to help figure the supply cost total.

The second step to Method A is to figure the cost or value of your time. This may actually necessitate keeping a journal as you work, jotting down start and stop times. If you are "mass producing" a craft you could even use a stop watch to time the placement or completion of each piece.

Take this total time for one piece and multiply it by how much your time is worth. You can base this on how much per hour you used to make at you "other" job OR you can subtract from this hourly rate based on the fact that you are now having more "fun" at your art "job" and would gladly do it for free (but try not to) OR you can add to this hourly rate because you have taken very expensive workshops and classes to learn your new art skill. Perhaps you are now working at something that no one else can do. My husband often tells me that people are not just paying for my artwork but are inadvertently paying for my skill, my knowledge, and my expertise. Don't sell yourself short. Once you have your hourly rate, multiply this rate to the time it took to create that piece.

Now you have your hourly rate for one piece and the cost of supplies for one piece. Step three is to add these two figures together and you'll get a rough but simple bottom line that may reveal worlds of information ("I'm doing this for THAT little amount of money?" or "No wonder no one wants to buy my work!"). You can also figure this on multiples being created at the same time. (The cost of 10 items' supplies plus the value of the time it took to make 10 items)

Let's walk through an example: Take out pencil and paper or just scribble in the margins (RAD) as we create the 20 items we mentioned above using $40 worth of supplies. We've figured, also, that the time it took to make one item was 30 minutes.   Our old job paid $15 per hour so our time is worth at least $7.50 for that 30 minutes. Our formula is

110

SUPPLY COST + HOURLY RATE=BOTTOM LINE

So in this case, $2 + $7.50 = $9.50. Getting $9.50 for the item means I have broke even. As mentioned in Chapter 6/Step 6, if we want more from that bottom line like a return on our investment, some fun money or any amount of profit, then we would need to adjust our prices accordingly.

Now take out pencil and paper (or work in the margins as we walk through a little more complicated scenario. (RAD)

Our example this time is for sculptures made from found materials. People throw out trash and let's say you are able to hammer and nail and glue this trash together in an attractive manner. All your friends and family like these works of art, so you've decided to sell your work to the public.

Your supplies cost $0 BUT your glue and nails for each piece take about 1/10th of a bottle or box to the tune of about .75 per project. Paint and varnish take about 1/3rd of a $10 container for a total of about $3.33 per project. It takes you an hour to create one piece and you feel like, even though you'd do it for free, your time should be worth something so you figure a conservative $10 for the hour. That may sound like all there is BUT did you think about the gas money to drive around to see what people throw out? You may figure that you spend one afternoon a week driving around for about 25 miles and at the publishing of this book that may equate to about $2.50 in gas money. You are also selling at a crafts' fair where your booth costs $50 for the day and you have 50 pieces to sell so it costs about $1 for that exposure. Your total now is about $17.58 to make that piece. I would round it up to $18 to compensate for miscellaneous supplies like the paper you used to print the price tags, some hand lettered signage, and table skirts for the booth display. In the world of retail or if you are attempting to make some fun money or more from these projects, you might want to double or triple that amount for a profit margin from $36 or $54. You can take the medium of these two prices ($45) or charge anywhere in between. Seriously assess the market and the quality of your work for the final decision. If this doesn't fit or feel right try Method B.

Method B to find your "bottom line" also includes a formula. This formula can help you get to the bottom line very objectively. Take out pencil and paper and work through these scenarios and you'll see the differences between method A and method B. (RAD)

Let's say that for a painting, you have found that the canvas and portion of paint used only costs $20 but you spent 100 man hours on the piece. Multiplied times a conservative $10 per hour and by using Method A, you would need $1020 just to break even. Can you see how things might start to get a little more complicated? If $1020 doesn't sound or feel like a good price, can you take less as an unknown artist and just enjoy the pleasure of painting? Or, are you selling you work in a profitable art oriented city or a small town in mid America so that $1020 sounds just about right? And finally is your work REALLY that good or better than the $1020 you figured? There could be lots of emotion involved in adjusting

112

your pricing leaving you inconsistent and unable to adjust your prices easily with Method A.

So, with Method B, you will first check out comparable prices for comparable items in the venues in which you intend to sell (RAD). As you note these prices, be sure to get some accurate measurements of these items. Sometimes this measurement can be found on the price tag or price listing sheet or you might be allowed to actually measure the piece with permission of the venue owner. Then, take out pencil and paper again, and work through this example:

Let's say you find that a 16" X 20" painting on average sells for $320 in the venue of your choice. If you were to multiply to get the square inches of the painting you would find that 16 X 20 = 320 square inches. You quickly see that the painting is selling for $1 per square inch. We're going to figure no commission is being paid to this gallery or shop (what a deal!) for the sake of learning our formula and later in this chapter we'll talk more about how your bottom line is effected with commissions. For our sculpture example, we'll stay in this no commission gallery and roughly measure some of the sculptures there to get the cubic inches (rather than square inches like a 2D painting). For our example, we find that an 8" X 4" X 3" sculpture that is 96 cubic inches is selling for $100 which means it is being sold for $1.04 per cubic inch (or perhaps the sculpture was figured at $1 per cubic inch for a total of $96 and just rounded up to make a better price point – more on this later).

So the formula for Method B is:

SIZE x SELECTED PRICE PER SQUARE (OR CUBIC INCH) = BOTTOM LINE

Remember that both of the examples for Methods A and B have not taken into account a gallery or retail shop's commission. For each type of art or craft there are some specific objectives upon which you need to focus your pricing no matter if you choose Method A, B or create a method or formula unique to your own art.

Specific Pricing for Craft items

For craft items, Method A works well. Once you have figured out your supply costs and time it took to create each item you have created your bottom line. From this bottom line, see if you can at least double this amount to make a decent retail price. Doubling the price is often the formula that retail establishments use so this is a good starting point.

Now check this retail price very objectively. Think like a customer. If you saw the item would you buy it at this price? Would you think, as many of your customers would, that "I could make that myself for less?" If your work is really that easy to duplicate, maybe you need to re-think your craft or its' price. Perhaps you could make it a little more special or unique by adding something or maybe you could upscale the

114

raw materials.

From your retail price, if someone were to offer to purchase several items and want a "deal", could you afford to take less per item? If you could, you might be able to establish a wholesale price which could be somewhat higher than your bottom line but below your retail price. Once your bottom is figured you have a solid base upon which to figure other prices, adjust prices, and hold your ground for less than fair "deals".

For example: (RAD with paper and pencil) Let's say you make a "thingy" with $4.50 worth of supplies. This "thingy" also takes about 15 minutes of your time to create. You figure your time is worth $12 per hour so you'll add $3 to the $4.50 for a total of $7.50 so far per item. The package for the "thingy" is a box and you found a bunch of boxes on sale for .10 each but they are normally .25 each. To be safe, add the .25 instead of the .10. So now our total is $7.75. If you are going to sell this item yourself at a show, how much is the booth rental and the divided cost of the display items you'll need like tables and tablecloths, signage and tags? You'll take a portion of this total and add it to your price. For our example, we're chosen to use our own old tables and display items but the booth rent is $50 for two days. I'll need to divide $50 by the number of items I have for sale (assuming each item is taking up approximately the same space in the booth – you'll have to adjust for larger or smaller items). For simplicity's sake I figure with 50 items, each item "costs" me $1 to set it up to sell for the two days. Added to my total I'm up to $8.75.   This $8.75 pays me back for all my time and supplies.   If I want to make a profit I'll need to attempt to double that price or more.   Doubling brings the total retail price to $17.50.   I can round this up to $18.00 or down to $17.00. If you round up or down to an even number for a craft/art show you won't have to worry about so much change but if you keep the .50 or .75 to your price you'll find it a good psychological price point.   Customers will feel that something like $19.50 is good because it's not a full $20 and/or will feel like $15.50 is just $15.   The .50 or .75 also makes it easy to have the customer feel like they got a small "deal" if you say "Let's just make it an even $15".   This also applies to larger amounts like having customers favor $775 over $800. But forget about the $11.99 or $11.95 – people are "on" to that. Also, attempting to add cents to a three or four figure price (hundreds and thousands) just confuses the issue.   Through a typo a friend of mine got lots of interest but no sales on her $11,0050 piece when it should have read $1,100.50.

Let's go back to our "thingy" example.   You've checked the market and you figure that $17.50 is a good price point so you go for it.   At the craft show if the day goes good, the $17.50 works well and hopefully you have enough quarters with you to make change.   If not, you are the "owner" of this "shop" and can make the call. Perhaps you can let someone have two items for $30 or sell one for $17 if you run out of change. You still know that $8.75 is your bottom line price so anything above that is a profit.   At the end of a bad day, knowing $8.75 is your bottom line, you can   lower the prices if
116

necessary but you'll know not to go below the $8.75 or you will be at a loss. If you sell out early, have you figured how much higher you can go for the next show? No fair raising prices at the same show but lowering prices is OK.

If this same "thingy" item is going to go directly to a retail store, can it be sold to the customer through that store for as much as $35.00? The shop owner must make some sort of profit. If they buy 10 items from you at $17 each, they may attempt to double that price to sell in their shop. Most time, however, they will want to buy several of the items from you at a "wholesale price". Do you have a wholesale price in mind somewhere between the $8.75 and $17.50? And if the store approaches you to sell on commission (meaning you'll agree to a percent of the sale only after the sale is made) are you prepared with proper paperwork and a good inventory of the pieces they'll have in their possession?

All of these prices have to be readily available in your mind or you need to be able to figure them quickly. There's often no time to "get back with you later" with a retailer who is in town for this show only and will take everything you've got at the right price if you can pack it up before he leaves that night. Knowing your bottom line, even if you have to grab a pencil and paper, you can do some easy math to sell out and start your fabulous art career. AND here's a neat little trick I use when there's just too many items and too many bottom lines for each item to remember off the top of my head – I use a code like an inventory number that secretly tells me my bottom line for each item so I can negotiate on the spot. For

117

example, if the item's bottom line is $8.75, the price tags reads something line ID#578, Price - $35.00.   With the numbers of my bottom line   written backward on the price tag and someone offering $6.00 for the item I know immediately that it's a no-go.   Try your own system (RAD) using backwards numbers or alphabet letters or something equally as easy for you to know and for the customer to not find out.

Specific pricing for 2 D art

2D art sold at craft/art fairs or directly to the public can use either method A or B to get to the bottom line and then adjusted to make a profit.   Once you figure this bottom line price you will also adjust it accordingly for gallery or shop representation where a commission is involved.

Let's review a couple of bottom line examples (RAD) If you price like we figured for crafts using Method A, a canvas might have cost you $10 and the paint to paint a 16" X 20" might be just a portion of a couple of tubes of paint probably totaling no more than $3.   If it only took you an hour to paint and you figure your time to be worth roughly $10 per hour, then your total cost to create the work might be as low as $23.   If you sell at this price you're profit margin is your hourly rate.   If the painting took as much as a week and/or about 40 hours to paint, then the price of $413 (or rounded to $415) might be your "sell directly to the public" price.

Or, if you figure your time to be worth as much as $100 per hour then a 16" X 20" painting that took 2 total hours to create would have a bottom line of about $213 in time and supplies. You can round your price down to $200 or up to $225 if you are selling directly to the public. Notice, also, that for 2 D artwork, this bottom line price of time plus materials is often your direct selling price. You may not need to double or triple the bottom line because you are making all your profit from the time involved to create the piece. But it's your pricing so if you think the market or your artwork deserves it, double or triple away.

So you see how these numbers can be hugely varied based on how much you consider your time to be worth or what the market will bear for your work. Your emotions may get heavily involved in this Method A for 2D art especially as you seriously analyze your renown (unknown artists' work shouldn't cost as much as well known artists' work) and how much you really enjoy working/creating. Even though you made $75 per hour in the corporate world, your retirement/current monetary position in life may mean you can take much less per hour just for the shear fun of your new "job" of creating OR you may have been laid off and are in desperate need to get even more for your hourly wage no matter how much time your artwork took to create. And you may have become particularly attached to your work (a huge "no-no" for a selling artist).

If your emotions are running high on Method A's figuring, Method B may work better for you. Use of Method B will help keep your emotions out of the picture (literally) and keep your prices more consistent.

For example, take out pencil and paper and RAD. Let's say you find that most 16" X 20" paintings done by comparable artists are selling on average, for about $500. If you multiply 16" X 20" you will have a total of 320 square inches in the painting. Divide $500 by 320 and the answer is $1.5625 meaning that the piece is priced at about $1.56 per square inch. If you multiply 320 square inches by $1.56 per square inch, this gives you the sale price of $499.20 which, rounded up, becomes $500. This could be the price that you choose to use to sell directly to the public remembering that the profit doesn't necessarily come from doubling or tripling of the bottom line unless you feel the market will bear it or if a commission is involved.

With these formulas we are also assuming that you are not paying anything extra or excessive for your supplies. You are using a standard canvas with your everyday acrylic or oil paint. If you used real gold leaf on your canvas or an excessive amount of modeling paste or varnish or you have a particularly expensive frame, you will need to adjust your price but the formula helps to keep your emotions out of the process, makes it easy to figure if someone wants to commission a different size and makes it quick to adjust for a gallery or retail establishment that wants to buy multiples or wants to buy your work outright rather than sell it based on commission.

Now using this formula and if there is no extra cost to the supplies means that every 16" X 20" is going to be priced the same. Having all your artwork with the same prices per size sort of sounds like being a used car salesman "take your

120

pick, ladies and gentlemen, any car on the lot - $1995") OR it can make a selection easier for the customer ("I really need a 16" X 20" over my couch and since they are all priced the same I can just pick my favorite"). If you really spent a lot of time and energy on one 16" X 20" over another 16" X 20", just as you did when you used more expensive supplies, you are more than welcome to add a little more to the price. It's your artwork and your livelihood so just be happy with your price. You are well aware of your bottom line so that you never have to settle for a loss.

Once you have a formula that you like to use, let's say you have been contacted by a particular retail store or gallery that wants to sell you work. You know what you want for your artwork but they don't want to buy it outright, they want to have a show or hang the piece in their shop and take a commission from the sale.   Let's run through some examples and ways to get your price easily in a situation where a commission upon sale is involved: (RAD)

Here's a relatively easy one.   Let's assume that a gallery that wants your work is taking 50% of the sale price. That means that if you and the gallery owner/rep sell a 16" X 20" piece of yours for $500 then you are   actually getting $250.   50% is easy to figure but let's try a more difficult commission. Use this formula for figuring your sale price and take home price when a   commission is to be taken out:

THE AMOUNT YOU WANT TO TAKE HOME divided by THE PERCENT YOU WILL GET = THE SALE PRICE

Work through this example to see how it works (RAD). We'll use the same 16" X 20" which is 320 square inches. If you want .75 per square inch then you figure that if you sold directly to the public you would charge $240 for this piece. Let's say, however that you want to sell this piece in a gallery or retail shop that is going to take 40% of the sale. How do you figure what they should charge or what should be the retail price so that you go home with your $240? What if they've put you on the spot and asked you what you want to sell the piece for? If you blurt out $240, you just lost $96 because they are going to take 40% for their sales commission. So how can you figure the sale price?

Using the formula you would take the $240 that you want for this piece, divide by .60 (the 60% that you would take home) and the answer would be 399.44262. Round that up to $400. If the gallery sold the piece for $400 they would take out their 40% commission of $160. Subtracting $160 from the $400 leaves you the $240 that you wanted.

What if the gallery is the one that wants the 60% and you will get 40%? Apply the formula and you will see that $240 (the amount you want for this piece) divided by .40 (the percent that you will get) is $600. If the gallery sells the piece for $600 and takes their 60% ($360) you will get your $240.

It helps to know these figures in order to price your pieces competitively and to keep yourself from shock when that commission gets subtracted.

As you travel you'll also notice how the square inch amount varies according to the public's interest in art in that particular area.   I have found the   square inch amount for a town like Memphis, Tennessee, (a more music oriented than art oriented city) averages about $1 per square inch at the writing of this book versus $1.50 to $2 per square inch in galleries in Atlanta, Georgia or Chicago, Illinois. In an art inspired community like Naples, Florida, Santa Fe, New Mexico or New York City, the price per square inch could be $3 or more.

Experiment with various amounts per square inch   on your own artwork and then apply that amount to various commissions that could be taken out. (RAD)

And here's an easy trick to make these figures easier with which to deal.   If you are struggling to figure your price or bottom line by multiplying by $1.26 or .96, make it easier on yourself by rounding this square inch amount up or down and you'll be able to adjust prices at the drop of a hat, almost off the top of your head.

For example: If you have found comparable square inch amounts to be .78 or 1.27 or some odd amount like that, just set in motion your multiplication table as .75 per square inch or 1.25.   Then an 8" X 10" (80 square inches) would be $60 (at .75 per square inch) or $80 (at 1.25 per square inch), a 16" X 20" would be $240 or $400.   That's a whole lot easier that trying to multiply .78 or 1.27 in you head.   A really easy figure to use is $1 per square inch (if your market can work with this amount).   Figuring $1 per square inch gives you $80 for an 8" X 10" (exactly what the square inches are), $320 for a 16"X 20", $480 for a 20" X 24", etc. Keeping your square inch amounts in easy/even increments will also allow you to quickly and easily figure odd size commissioned pieces. "Oh, you want a 22" X 36"? That will run you about $800 (rounded up from $792 at $1 per square inch)." Even if you have to take pencil and paper or calculator, you can figure quickly and consistently. See how easily you can figure an odd size canvas with .25 per square inch or .75 or whatever you have chosen. (RAD) Try something outrageous like a 2" X 2" or a large 6' X 7'(that's feet not inches). (RAD)

For a photograph, a combination of the two methods to price paintings is useful. If you print a series of 8" X 10"'s and price them all at $80 then you have used the formula of $1 per square inch for your price. If you sell all of your 8" X 10" pieces for $80 each, take your pick, then they all take on a more mass produced feel. People already know that many prints can be made from one photographic image, but they'd rather think that the piece they bought is one of a kind. At an arts and craft show, you can use this "mass produced" pricing to your benefit when you have one of the 8" X 10"'s beautifully matted and framed for $375 or $400 and also offer sleeved copies for $80 each. People who love and are attracted to your booth by the gorgeous $400 piece, but don't have $400 in their budget to spend, may just as well take home one or more $80 sleeved copies. And just like in the case of paintings that you've put more effort into, you may need to adjust prices of like-sized pieces according to things like: Didn't it take a lot of danger to hang from that cliff to get that particular shot versus the ease of taking a picture of a   flower from your garden?   How about that series of photos from your African trip?   Didn't the trip add some cost to the ability to capture those shots?   If you are the one selling directly to the customer, the various pricing differences can give you a chance to tell the story behind the artwork.   From the story, comes the sale.   "Why is this 8" X 10" more than that one? Well, let me tell you about the three day trek into the jungle to find that specific flower."

In addition to the cost of   your photographs, for proper presentation you have often invested quite a lot in mats, frames and glass.   Be sure to recoup these expenses. That means that in many cases it's not so much the cost of the print but the cost of the framing that raises the price.   As I'll tell you in the section on Presentation, the more uniform your frames, the better, so if you can order or buy in bulk do so, selecting all your mats and frames in the same style or colors so that they won't detract from your photos. This not only saves you some money but it also makes your work look much more professional.

Specific pricing for 3D art

I hope you read all the information about pricing for 2D art even if you thought it didn't apply because it sure did.   The only thing you have to change in the information and formulas

125

for 2D artwork is in multiplying by cubic inch instead of square inch. You will also adjust your price according to the materials you use. A set formula of $1 per cubic inch for a limestone sculpture may change to $4 per cubic inch for copper or marble. And, again, it's your livelihood so adjust according to your needs, the market reactions and the locality of your sales.

For all types of artwork, as you get more sales and increased demand for your work, as you begin to sell in better venues, you can increase your prices. But as a beginning or unknown artist it's best to take your chances and test the waters on the lower end of the price scale. You can always go up in price but going down in price not only hurts your reputation but it's going to hurt your feelings too and may wrongly convince you to drop out of the market altogether before you even get a starting chance.

PRESENTATION

I'm often asked to lecture art groups in seminars and workshops about the presentation of their artwork. I usually title my speech "Presenting Your Art, Presenting Yourself – A guide to showcasing your artwork to everyone from friends to jurors, from local art shows to major art galleries" and I usually bring along some examples to show both the good and bad of presentations that I and my fellow art gallery owners and jurors have seen.

I begin my presentation by having everyone cross their arms. This is a psychological body language move that shows the closed mindedness of many people to whom they might present their art. Many gallery owners take this stance when an artist walks in the door. It's not that they don't want to see your art, but they are often extremely busy and not in the frame of mind to see you or your artwork right then. Even if you give a gift of your artwork to a friend or neighbor, unless they have asked for your work, their initial thoughts may be "what am I supposed to do with this? I love their work but this is just the wrong size/color/theme for my home/office".

As I talk about presenting your artwork I also emphasize the presentation of yourself to these possible "closed minded" people. Many times you are selling the "sizzle" (yourself) along with the steak (your artwork). Gone are the days of the hungry starving artist. Gallery owners and buyers of your work would like to think that you are successful and therefore the artwork they buy or represent is equally as successful. There are some specific tips and tricks that work best for selling both the "sizzle" and the "steak". . .

To Friends and Family

Sizzle-wise, your friends and neighbors already know you well so there's no reason to present yourself as something other than what they know and love. The steak (your artwork) is what you need to concentrate on in this presentation.

First, they have raved about your work but, after all, they are your friends, so are they just saying this to be nice? Don't just assume that they would love to have a piece of your artwork. They might not, and then they are obligated to take it and make an emergency hanging when they see you walk up their front walk for a visit. Maybe it's not so much that they didn't like the piece or don't really like your work, but it could be that it's just not the right color or size. Plus your friend's and family's taste in art may not be your taste. So my suggestion when it comes to friends and family is to never give them a piece unless they've asked for a specific piece AND if you are really making your living from the sale of your artwork NEVER just give it away. You can always tell them how flattered you are that they would like to have one of your pieces and that you'll be glad to give them the "friends and family discount". You may both laugh at that but you should seriously have in mind what you bottom line price is and at least get your cost out of the piece. Perhaps you could barter for something in exchange. "I really wouldn't feel right charging you for this piece you love, but you're wife makes great pecan pies, maybe we can swap?"

Once you've decided to swap or discount a piece to friends or family, make sure they know that you've presented them with this present/gift/deal and that you don't just do this for just anyone. There's no need for them to brag about the "deal" they got.

The best tip for presenting pleasing artwork to friends

or family is to either give gift certificates for a discount, gift certificates for a commissioned piece, or if you MUST give your work for free as a gift of promotional item, set out a selection of pieces, invite the receiver to view the pieces and allow them to pick out their favorite.

Craft and Art Shows

We've discussed the presentation of your artwork through your set up for craft and art shows but we need to be sure to mention a little more about selling the sizzle (yourself) at these shows.   As you study the shows that you want to attend, notice the look of the venders.   Watch how much attention the "artistic look" gets over the jeans and sweatshirt. As I mentioned, you can actually wear your product or don a t-shirt with your logo.   You can also dress artistically by covering your casual clothes with a painted apron (one that looks like it's really been in the studio) or some overalls with a paint brush or wood chisel sticking out of the pocket.   People like to brag about buying the piece from this "eccentric artist fellow" or   brag about how they bought this fabulous scarf right off the lady who was creating them.   You can also follow some of the ideas for dressing for art opening receptions.

Contests and Juried Shows

Most of the time, you won't be seen at all when you present your work for a contest or juried show and even if you did, no amount of preparation to present your "looks" will effect the judges decisions. For contests and juried shows where you will not be seen, you'll concentrate on the "steak" (your artwork) and not the sizzle of your charming smile.

Previously we spoke about the submission of your work for contests and juried shows. Once you have met therequirements for the entry selection, there will also be requirements for the presentation at the actual show even if it's an online show. Each show/contest/presentation will have a set of rules. You must follow these rules to the letter. I've even seen shows require a particular type of wire on the back of a painting that also had to be a specific number of inches from the top of the painting (including the slack of the wire). When things get this complicated it helps to have the piece professionally framed.

To get your piece safely to the display location, your artwork must be transported so that it will arrive in its' best shape and you should expect the work back (unless it sells) in equally good shape. Though a contest, show location, gallery or shop often has you sign a waver releasing them from damage to your work you should expect that they would take reasonable care and you can help make this possible.

First of all, if you are hand delivering the piece some suggested transport materials would be bubble wrap, tissues, and /or plastic sleeves. Important tips include NOT using newspapers (the print is prone to leaving ink on your piece) or Styrofoam peanuts (don't you just hate those things). A nifty trick for 2D art is "noodles" or those foam insulation tubes that plumbers use for pipes. Slit one side of the tube, cut it to length, and slide it over the edge of a painting or panel. Once in place, you can stack paintings right on top of each other. If you create something that you want the venue to use for repacking, put your name on the packing material and make it easy to reuse. Don't just tape it to death so that removal of the piece requires cutting tape, ripping plastic, etc. Rather, tape your plastic into the form of a sleeve that they can easily store and repack. Include a sack or box (unless the piece is already in a box) for them to store your packing material for re-use. If it's there, they'll probably use it. If not, you take more chances with someone else packing your piece up using their own supplies.

Likewise, if you have to mail or ship your pieces, my first tip is to let the professionals do it – keeping in mind the cost that must be recouped upon sale of the piece. This is an expensive option but can mean your piece can be insured for damage in transit. If, however, you have the supplies and have seen someone actually pack a similar piece, you may find that you can ship pieces yourself for much less. BUT know what you are doing before you completely tape the box shut only to find that the postal service won't let you use duct tape or find that a wooden crate was a great idea until you found out the cost of shipping a 500 pound wooden crate is way more than what you needed to ship a 75 pound piece carefully wrapped in bubble wrap and cardboard. And remember, if your piece must be shipped back to you, many of the venues will charge return fees.

Coffee Shops, Library and Lobby Shows

Most of the time coffee shops, libraries, and/or lobbies don't care how you frame your work, what your work looks like, or how long you hang it. But you, on the other hand, should. They are just getting free decoration for their venue or the bragging rights for using their unused conference room. If you are striving to become more professional you can use these venues as a fabulous training ground.

Sizzle-wise, when you meet with the owner or manager of these places to ask for a show, look professional. The venue doesn't usually focus on the presentation of artwork but they are businesses that are used to working with professionals. You will meet and discuss things with them as a business professional, not as a paint covered artist.

Once they've decided to allow you a show, make sure you know all their rules. Though they may not think they have any, you need to make sure they will allow screws or do they just want nails used on the walls or neither (meaning only sticky tape and very light artwork) and what type of responsibilities do you have once you start hauling ladders in and possibly interrupting customer service? Once you understand their major "rules" you must use common sense to make the whole experience pleasant for all involved (does that heavy wall piece look like it's going to fall on a customer's head? Does the bathroom door open right into your free standing statue?)

As you bring in your artwork for display (hopefully during a slow time of a slow day – the owner can recommend a time) you'll want to   bring them in with all the pricing tags, signage (if allowed) and hanging supplies all in one day. Transport of the pieces can be found in our tips for shipping artwork but in this case you will need to take all of the packing supplies home with you.

Once transported to the space, my tip as a gallery owner who has hung more than 50 major one man and group shows is to lean the artwork along the floor as close as you can to where it will be hung.   You'll easily see where color selections need to be matched or spaced out, sizes need to be balanced, and heavy or odd shaped pieces need to be safely out of the way of traffic. You can measure between the pieces to easily space them horizontally. As you place them you will find that sometimes you will need a stud finder to assure that the wall above is going to be sturdy enough for the size, weight and shape of the piece that you want to hang there.   If presenting sculptures, you may even need Plexiglas covers or the use of niches, shelves, and out of the way corners, to safely arrange the   display of your work.   With pieces in place on the floor, you can proceed to nail, hammer,   and screw or place each piece. 2D artwork will be hung directly above the space where you had it placed it on the floor.   My tip for height is to hang the center or most predominant piece first. This piece can be hung just at random or carefully measured from the ceiling or floor to get the center of the piece at a common eye level.   If you are particularly tall or short remember that the center of the piece needs to be at eye level for an average size person.   Once you have the center or focal piece in place, you can then level all the other work to this piece (a laser leveler will come in handy here) or alternate the pattern of the hanging to balance the overall look.   The easiest hanging job can often be when all of the pieces are the same size like you might do for a show of nothing but 8" X 10" photographs.   If you have various size pieces, however, it needn't be too much harder. For example,   you could hang a   center piece highest with a piece on each side, both about 2 inches lower.   You can create exact symmetry like this or offset the pieces as you notice the one on the left must be hung above a 4' cabinet or some other obstruction.   Don't forget to   take advantage of various size walls or the arrangement of the furniture and accessories in the space. If you know that you are going to be able to   have a show at a particular location, say, 6 months in advance, you can even   create pieces specifically to fit an odd corner or nitch.

Once you have the opportunity to show, you will also be learning from this experience some valuable information on how to   advertise the event, plan a possible reception, and interact with your guests. Here's where all the presentation materials that we discussed in the packet for gallery

134

representation come into play. Your bio or artist's statement framed on the wall can explain your work when you can't be there, your business cards can be left by the cash register (the venue probably won't make sales for you, they'll just let customers contact you personally) and if you are allowed a show, you'll learn to design and order your postcards in time to invite your guests to see your work. Always allow yourself at least two months in advance to create these if you want plenty of time to order them, receive them, and get them in the mail. If you order any later, you can still get postcards as quickly as overnight but you'll pay extra in the shipping costs for your lack of planning time. You will also find that the media is very receptive to listing your show for free if you contact them soon enough (at least two – four weeks in advance). For written advertising, notice which sections of the paper or your local magazines list art shows. Then find out who is in charge of the art show listings. (RAD) Next, find out their requirements and deadlines. Once you have this information, you can usually keep addresses and submission requirements in your computer and/or submission deadlines on a monthly calendar. Once you have this information, contact them any time you do something noteworthy artistically. You are at their mercy when it comes to space (sometimes the art columns are cut out due to a huge music convention or other newsworthy event that week) but if you get listed, it's great free publicity. Sadly if your listing got cut or left out it can make or break the attendance at your show but with other means of advertising like signs at the venue, postcards, posters and anything else you want to use for publicity, you can survive. A trick I've learned when I get left out for my opening reception, is to advertise the show weekly (many times your contact person will feel bad about your being left out and list your show any other time they can) and/or have a "closing reception". A closing reception is the same as the opening reception only it's at the end of the show (the last weekend or even the last day). No matter what you want to advertise (a show, a class, an opening, etc) contact with the wrong person will fall on deaf ears so make every effort to find the proper listings and addresses and get to know these people, even if it's just a casual email thanking them for listing your show. And always give them a personal invitation. Another neat publicity "trick" is to write an article yourself and send photos to the news media. The article and/or picture can often be used as filler for the lifestyle sections of the paper or a magazine. Give it a try even if you don't consider yourself a great writer. All you have to do is to write in the third person and at least list the show, its' location, some people in attendance, or something unusual or newsworthy about the event. I once got a nice article due to a power outage on opening reception night. We took pictures of attendees viewing the work with hand held flashlights and got a nice photo and article to accompany it. Knowing the right contact people can also get you an opportunity for television interviews or human interest stories on the news. On a slow day, or if your show particularly interests them or is tied to another local event, you might find a whole camera crew show up offering you a great personal

136

appearance opportunity.

Back to the show, if the venue allows receptions, they may even offer to provide some of the reception food or drinks. On the other hand, they may not allow receptions at all or may have rules for the reception such as "no outside food" or "no alcohol". Follow these rules and you'll be asked back for another show. Don't follow their rules and this will be a one time event. Also, if you have food that people trampled into the floor or a guest that gets a little tipsy, you'll be barred not only from this venue but any other venues in the chain. You may even be charged a fee for clean up or repair. Anytime you put on a show for yourself, be aware of the "costs" and care of displaying in public. It might help on opening night to have a second pair of eyes for refilling trays and cleaning up. After all, you are supposed to be the guest artist, not the kitchen help. You don't need to be passing out canapés . . . you need to be talking about your artwork. A real classy way to have your own reception is to hire servers or a bartender. Remember that you are essentially "renting the hall" for free so just as the scouts would say, "leave the space in as good a shape as you found it".

During the opening reception you are selling the sizzle (yourself) even if most of your guests are well known to you. Just as they would look different in their "work clothes", you should look different in your part as an artist. As I've said before, the days of the starving artist and the look of the starving artist are over. Here are some tips and tricks for selling yourself along with your artwork as you make your presence known for shows and receptions:

1.   Do not clash with your artwork – wear pastels if you work is mostly pastels and bold colors if you work is bold – remember you may have lots of photos taken both for your use and for use in advertising the show.   How will you look standing next to a work of art?   My tip for not clashing is to dress completely in   neutrals or black.

2.   Dress business-like with an artistic flair – For women, dress as you would to go shopping in a high end store only add something kind of funky like a very artistic pin, a hand woven scarf (perhaps of your own making) or a funky pair of shoes.   For men, how about business casual (dress shirt or sports coat) with a splash of art in a colorful tie (possibly hand painted) or even a beret.   OK, so maybe the beret is not quite you, but I've seen men come across extremely artistic with a business-like look and a pair of shoes with a couple of drops of paint or some excess plaster on the tips.   The whole idea is to let someone know that you are a working artist and are a part of that artistic community.

3.   Dress differently – This is a really odd way to sell the sizzle but I've seen it work extremely well.   First, determine how you might expect your guests to dress.   If the event is anticipated to be a fancy affair and everyone will probably be in evening gowns or even tuxes, unless dress codes dictate, you could be dressed in jeans or a fabulous artistic gypsy-like cape.   If the affair is rather casual and you figure that most guests will be in summer vacation-type outfits (an outdoor show or vacation location) then you need to be dressed

138

up. You can go so far as to wear a sparkly cocktail dress or a tuxedo jacket. Sound crazy? The point of this way of dressing is to distinguish yourself from the crowd. ("Who's the guy in the tux?" "Oh, that's the artist") It's fun to sell the sizzle through your style of dress and you'll get a chance to really get your creative juices flowing if you want to "play" at fitting the part of the successful artist.

Organizations

Organizations have their own shows to try to help their members get more exposure and to learn how to be more professional but depending on the size or goals of the group, being in an organization's show may actually teach you worse habits. For example if everyone in a particular organization is an extreme amateur your work might slip into that amateur category either by association or because "everyone else had cheap frames so I didn't bother pulling out my best frame". I once had a group show of all of the artists I currently represented in the gallery. I had two or three very successful professional artists who were going to be showing their work alongside some very beginner-type artists. The hanging of the show was extremely crucial for if I showed a very professional piece with a high price tag next to a poorly framed, more amateur piece, it did not raise the value of the amateur piece but rather, lowered the value of the professional piece.

There is an ad I found in a magazine once that was a

139

two page spread.   On the left hand page was a painting sitting in an attic leaning against a broken chair.   It was dusty and had cobwebs, leftover Christmas ornaments, boxes of junk, etc all around it.   The caption read "Painting - $25".   On the right hand page was the exact same painting hung on a gallery wall. There was lots of space around the painting, proper lighting, and even a velvet rope to keep the admirers from touching what looked like a masterpiece.   The caption read "Painting - $25,000".

Without trying to be a snob, if your organization is basically   just the local watercolor class then maybe you need to exhibit a playful watercolor study, simply framed, or a pack of hand painted watercolor note cards for this show and save the intensely executed, elaborately framed   landscape for another show with another group or venue.   Maybe it's time to enjoy the camaraderie of this smaller group but save your artwork for a larger more professional group.   It all comes down to how you feel about being a big frog in a little pool or a little frog in a big pool. Are you ready for greater challenges in shows are do you like to collect tons of dime store blue ribbons because you're always the best in the small local show?

Likewise,   the sizzle or look of your fellow members can inspire you.   Once you begin to learn who does   what type artwork and how successful they are with their art, you'll notice a type of dress or style they wear.   Do not emulate these people but use your RAD to see what they may be consciously or unconsciously saying as far as the selling of their art is concerned.   Remember that an organization is mostly about promoting the artwork, not the artist (just like the old art schools who taught everything about creating and nothing about selling).   Notice that if the artist is highly successful in sales but still dresses like an artistic "bum" perhaps it works for them but unless their reputation proceeds them, imagine the gallery owner's first impression.   Seeing this particular artist before they were aware of the artwork might have closed a door too early.   AND if this successful artist dressed successfully, how much more art might they sell?   Likewise, does the little old blue haired lady in the group look like she would be creating Grandma Moses type paintings or cutting edge abstracts?   As a first time selling artist, you may have a first impression barrier to overcome and who needs any more barriers to the sale of our artwork?   Making silent observations like this with your fellow organization members can be a real learning experience while you still benefit from networking with these individuals.

Retail and Art Galleries

In retail shops, your "sizzle" is a huge presentation point. Up to now, jurors, people who select your pieces for the small shows and even the coffee shops and libraries didn't pay much attention to your "looks".   Your artwork or simply the fact that they needed some art on the walls was all they cared about.   In the case of a juried show, they may never see you except on opening night. Retail and professional galleries for that matter, will see you first and care about how you look (whether they admit it or not). Now I'm not saying they are looking for fashion models. But they are looking for a certain level of professionalism or mystique. The days of the starving artist are definitely over for them. They want to promote successful artists.

Take for example the exercise I have my lecture groups do where they cross their arms. They are acting as shop or gallery owners who are obviously   not open to seeing your work. Now,   let's say you come bounding up to their desk in your vacation/leisure clothes.   First, they will think you are a customer and their adrenaline for a sale gets to pumping. As soon as you say that you are an artist,   they are already disappointed.   That's not a great way to make a first impression.   Likewise if you are all dolled up with your finest jewelry or wearing a nice   suit, once they find out you are an artist, the vision of a possible sale   vanishes from their minds in a huge wave of disappointment.   So what is the best way to approach retail or gallery owners?   Assuming that you have visited the gallery or shop you already know how to look if you were going to be a customer.   Take your dress code from this point and   "artsy it up" a bit. Refer to the ideas for dressing at opening receptions for some suggestions.   Basically,   "Be Memorable" needs to be your motto. Watch the movies and see what the "artist" is supposed to look like and emulate that. And introduce yourself as an artist as soon as you can so they will be in the proper frame of mind to give you their undivided attention (hopefully if you want to talk shop you've even made an appointment so the appropriate representative is available).

Your artwork presentation for retail and/or an art gallery will be much the same for both venues. In framing there has been a drastic change in the past few years. The framing of a 2D piece used to involve the nicest and most expensive frame imaginable and if your work just screams for the need of a heavy expensive gold gilt frame, then so be it but now a days, don't be surprised if the gallery or retail establishment calls you up saying they've got a buyer but the buyer doesn't like the frame. Would you discount the piece and take the frame off? I've had artists in my gallery who refuse to remove the frame and I've even heard of one artist in New York that considers his hand made frames part of the artwork to the point that you must sign an agreement upon purchase that you will not take the frame off the piece. But we're in this business to make sales. Why make people jump through hoops to buy our work? Why be hard to get along with? And, why even go to all the expense of framing something when it's probably not going to suit the buyer anyway.

The best way to present 2D artwork is to let the artwork speak for itself. For photographs, this means neutral mats (black, white, or crème colored) with plain metal (black, silver or chrome) frames under glass or Plexiglas. The buyer can easily transport the piece, change the frames if necessary, or hang the piece as is, and most importantly, your artwork is what is most appealing to them, not some elaborate "work of art" frame. This will also help you in the expense column if you find a resource through which you can buy multiple

143

quantities of similar mats and frames and again, LET THE ARTWORK SPEAK FOR ITSELF. I can just about guarantee that no matter how great that photo looks in its' burgundy mat and ornate frame, it's going to be the wrong color or the frame is not going to match their décor. And a classy touch for a photo is to be able to sign the neutral mat or print the title of the piece on the mat right below the picture. As always, watch what the most successful photographers are doing and emulate their example.

Likewise for a painting, nine times out of ten the frame will be the wrong size, color, or style. Why go to all the hassle in the first place? My tip is to use gallery wrapped canvases for your paintings (the customer can frame or not frame as their décor dictates) or price the piece with frame optional. One of my pet peeves is ¾ inch stapled edge canvases hanging on a wall for sale. Unless these are grouped, they tend to look rather flimsy and the stapled edge has a very unfinished look. The buyer knows automatically that in addition to the price of the painting, that they will have the additional cost of a frame even before they can enjoy the piece. . An inexpensive trick that you can use with stapled edge canvases is to cut and paint 1" or wider wood lathing strips to fit each side. Tack these pieces with finishing nails to the stapled edges of the canvas giving the sides some substance to stand out against the wall. If the buyer likes the painting, the painted strips (a neutral color or color to match or accentuate the paintings) are a way to attractively hang the work immediately or can be easily popped off if the buyer would prefer to frame the piece. We call this

144

the "old college try" for as students, this form of framing was perfect for a tight budget and with matching neutral strips, made the artwork the focal point, not the framing LETTING THE ARTWORK SPEAK FOR ITSELF.

Lately a new feature seen in homes and galleries is with gallery wrapped canvases or wood panels with 1" or larger wooden sides which are sloppy from the artists' hard work on the piece. In other words, the sides have drips and smears and even fingerprints from the artist. These sloppy-sided pieces are hanging and being sold in some of the most exclusive galleries in the world. Again, it's all about the artwork so back to step 5, build a successful body of work, and often, everything else will fall into place. (RAD)

For sculptures and 3D work, just be sure the shop or gallery displays the up side up and the down side down and that the piece is shown in its' best light or direction. I'm reminded of the bag of "trash" that was thrown out of a major New York gallery which proved later to have been the focal point of a very expensive show.

Websites

With the anonymous aspect of a website you can be a mysterious "no picture" artist or splash a wonderful "cover art" type photo of yourself predominately on page one or the bio page of your website. I have women artist friends who keep

145

themselves anonymous by painting under the initials of their names. They have no picture on their website to prove that they are a woman because they are under the impression that men artists sell better than women artists (don't get me started). Then, there are those who have this wonderful photo of themselves in this fabulous art studio or painting on the banks of the Thames. Remember that a photo can be worth a thousand words so look around for a place or outfit in which you can create the artist "mystique".

Presentation of your artwork on a website can be found in Chapter 7. If you have chosen to photograph your own work make sure to use a neutral background like a black sheet hung on the wall which drapes under your sculpture or crop out the wall around a painting. Other tricks to taking your own photos are to photograph your work before it's varnished so that there won't be such a glare in the picture, photographing it before it is framed, using an 8 mega pixel or higher camera, and using proper lighting. Workshops and books will advise you best about the use of bounce lights or outdoor lighting. If your own personal photography comes out less than you expected or if the colors are not satisfactory, I highly recommend professional photography. Pictures for your own inventory may be of a lesser quality but anything presented to the public needs to be extremely accurate AND in many instances your work will be compared to others. Don't let the photo be the only thing that knocked you out of a selection process. It's all about having excellent photos. Your website itself, even if it doesn't result in sales will most likely lead to shows, full classes, seminars or workshop dates but only if your work looks good on the site.   Use the websites as a way to "open your studio" to interested buyers.   Use the same information that you compiled for your gallery submission packets to interest them in you, your work, and where it can be found.

Chapter 9: What Now?

So now you're an artist.   Everything about you from your personal appearance to your body of work says you are an artist.   Your reputation is beginning to precede you.   Now what?

Author Jack White says that having the job of artist means that only one thing can make you lose your job and that is if the public "fires" you.   How do they fire you?   By not buying your work.   What keeps them from not buying your work? Maybe they have no idea that you are an artist.   Can you say, "I am an artist?" and create that artist mystique? Maybe they can't find you.   Are you promoting yourself? Maybe your work doesn't interest them. Do you have a style? Are you painting what the customer wants or still determined to be a "starving artist" painting only what you want when you want it? Are you painting blue daisies even though no one wants blue daisies until you essentially turn blue? Maybe the public   thinks you aren't interested in them?   Do you respond to their inquiries? Do you have them on your mailing list for shows?

If you've done everything you know how to do from the ideas in The Seven Steps of Selling Your Artwork,   if you've explored every idea from every   class, lecture, workshop, and conversation that you've experienced, if you've applied RAD over and over again and if you're still not selling or enjoying the selling of your artwork, you can still be passionate about its' creation.   The business of art is going to take a stretch of the left brain in a right brained endeavor but the beauty of successfully selling your art is making that 9:00 – 5:00 workday become a 9:00 – 5:00 creation day.   Enjoying what you do whether it's just the act of creation or the creation and selling of your artwork, will add 5 days to your weekend.

Here's to your success both as a creator and as a seller. Enjoy the ride as much as the destination.

Appendix and Resources

Suggested History books:

       History of Art by H. W. Janson

       History of Art for Young People by H. W. Janson

       The Story of Painting by Sister Wendy Beckett

Suggested Arts Magazines:

       Professional Artist Magazine

       Sunshine Artist Magazine

       The Artists' Magazine

Reference material:

       The Magic of Selling Art by Jack White

       Artist's & Graphic Designer's Market

       The Art Game by Robert Wraight

       StoreSupply.com

       VistaPrint.com

Example of a Query Letter:

Specific Gallery Name
Specific contact person and title if available
Street Address
City, State   Zip Code

Dear(proper name of contact person or "Gallery Director"),

I recently visited your gallery and enjoyed viewing your represented artwork. As an artist, I would like the opportunity to show you some of my current landscape paintings for your consideration.

Enclosed you will find further information about me, my artwork, and contact information in hopes that we may be able to set up a convenient time for a personal interview and viewing of my artwork.

I look forward to hearing from you and will call next week to confirm your receipt of this packet.

Thank you for your consideration.
 Your signature
 Your name typed

Example of an Artist's Bio

Answers: Who are You?

Often written in third person

The artist, Jane M. Croy was born and raised in the South with a passion for drawing and painting. Majoring in art in both high school and college, Jane earned both a Bachelors Degree in Art and a Masters Degree of Art in Teaching from the University of Memphis in Memphis, Tennessee.

Jane immediately began her art career as an art teacher in the Memphis City and Shelby County School Systems. Here she taught as many as 150 students per day inspiring junior high aged students to create and understand the basics and fun of all art techniques.

After 13 years, Jane left the field of teaching to become a   professional artist. Through a representative, she began her career selling an average of one painting per week for three years to individuals, galleries, and retail shops from Naples, Florida to Chicago, Illinois.

Jane began self representation to increase the value of her work and to have more control over its distribution. By opening her own art gallery in her hometown of Memphis, Tennessee she often sold pieces still wet on the canvas as she both worked the gallery and kept up her gallery/studio area in the same location.

Jane's passion for teaching and for leading and helping other artists was fulfilled with the expansion of the gallery to include struggling beginner artists whose work and promotion were fine tuned and guided through Jane's tutoring, guiding and mentoring.

Currently Jane teaches classes in painting for beginners to advanced students in acrylic and oil. She is also available for workshops in painting techniques and in the marketing of artwork for both artists and art related businesses. Most recently Jane has been in demand for seminars, lectures, and private coaching for art careers and well as for demonstrations of her own painting styles and techniques.

Artwork by J. M. Croy can be found in homes throughout the United States and in England. In addition to her impressionistic and abstract artwork, Jane accepts commissions for realistic pastel and oil portraits.

Example of an Artist's Statement

Written in first person

      As a child, I remember walking through the fields with my grandfather as he told me Indian legends about the landscape features and animals we saw.   He passed his Cherokee heritage on to me and I relate many of his stories through my artwork.   The colors I use are as symbolic as the Indian symbols I depict in each painting.   I often dream the colors of the paintings before I begin the actual work, creating a greater understanding of the influence of my Indian ancestors.   Though my grandfather is no longer with me, his presence is felt every time I pick up a paintbrush.

Artist's Resume

(use the template for a regular job application resume)

    Name

    Address

    Phone number

    Website

    E-mail address

Education

    Elementary School

    College/Technical School:

    Degrees earned or course of study

    Art Classes (particularly if you took classes with well known artists or teachers)

    Current Employment (Optional – use only if it relates to art)

    Awards and Honors

(You can include copies of articles about you or your work/shows in your application packet))

    Group shows

    Solo Exhibitions

    Permanent collections (museums, corporations, or murals)

    Membership in organizations plus offices you held

    Other: Title this and successive sections according to the information included such as:

        Workshops you have led

        Books you have written

        Classes you have taught

Example of an Agreement Form

Date _____

This agreement is between the artist, (fill in your name), and_____(name of selling venue)_____ to be known as "seller".

Seller agrees to take reasonable care in the showing and sale of the artwork listed below. Upon sale of each piece artist agrees to a commission of : _____% to be paid to the seller.

Artist further (agrees/disagrees) allowance of the removal of pieces from the seller's location for approval.

This agreement will be in effect from _____ to _____ at which time all artwork listed below which has not been sold and/or accounted for will be returned to the artist.

Title of pieces   Description of pieces   Sale Price

(Use as much space or number of columns as necessary)

Signature of Owner/Seller/Representative   Date

_____   _____

Signature of Artist

_____   _____

(You can add/delete anything in an agreement to cover all your expenses and desires. Though morally binding, it is not a legal document but makes the seller aware of your interests and concerns.)

www.ingramcontent.com/pod-product-compliance
Lightning Source LLC
Chambersburg PA
CBHW051523170526
45165CB00002B/586